Social Skills

Improve Your Social Skills

Build Self-Confidence, Manage Shyness & Make Friends

Bill Andrews

☐ **_Copyright 2018 by Bill Andrews - All Rights Reserved._**

This document is geared towards providing exact and reliable information in regards to the topic and issue covered. The publication is sold with the idea that the publisher is not required to render accounting, officially permitted, or otherwise, qualified services. If advice is necessary, legal or professional, a practiced individual in the profession should be ordered.

- From a Declaration of Principles which was accepted and approved equally by a Committee of the American Bar Association and a Committee of Publishers and Associations.

In no way is it legal to reproduce, duplicate, or transmit any part of this document in either electronic means or in printed format. Recording of this publication is strictly prohibited and any storage of this document is not allowed unless with written permission from the publisher. All rights reserved.

The information provided herein is stated to be truthful and consistent, in that any liability, in terms of inattention or otherwise, by any usage or abuse of any policies, processes, or directions contained within is the solitary and utter responsibility of the recipient reader. Under no circumstances will any legal responsibility or blame be held against the publisher for any reparation, damages, or monetary loss due to the information herein, either directly or indirectly.

Respective authors own all copyrights not held by the publisher.

The information herein is offered for informational purposes solely and is universal as so. The presentation of the information is without contract or any type of guarantee assurance.

The trademarks that are used are without any consent, and the publication of the trademark is without permission or backing by the trademark owner. All trademarks and brands within this book are for clarifying purposes only and are the owned by the owners themselves, not affiliated with this document.

Table of Contents

Introduction 5

Chapter 1: Get Your Mind Right 8

Chapter 2: Get Ready To COMMIT 13

Chapter 3: Get Ready To Go On A Journey 20

Chapter 4: Laying The Foundation For Enhanced Social Skills: The Importance Of Self-Confidence 25

Chapter 5: Improve Your Self-Esteem By Learning To Love Yourself 31

Chapter 6: Self-Acceptance Leads To Greater Self-Esteem 38

Chapter 7: What is Self-Confidence Anyway? 47

Chapter 8: Overcoming Shyness 67

Chapter 9: Getting Ready To Get Social 80

Chapter 10: Getting Into The Zone 89

Chapter 11: Speak Confidently 96

Chapter 12: Occupy The Same Emotional Space 107

Chapter 13: Tap the Power of Similarity 117

Chapter 14: Don't Underestimate The Power of Stories 121

Chapter 15: Set A Date and Do It 126

Conclusion 132

Introduction

If you want to live a happier, healthier and more fulfilling life, you're going to have to learn how to get along with others.

I know you probably already know this, this is probably something that you are trying to avoid. Maybe you're struggling in certain areas of your life and you know that you can stand a little bit more socialization. It's easy to spot the problem.

The reason why this should be so obvious to most people is that human beings are social animals. That's right. No matter how introverted you are or how shy you think you may be, deep down inside, you need other people. That's just how we're wired. This is part of the human condition. How come?

- ✓ We need other people to help us do things.
- ✓ We need other people to inspire us.
- ✓ We need others to give us the information we need to function or add value to the lives of others.

No matter how seemingly "isolated" a person is, he or she needs other people. That's the bottom line. If you're reading this book, you're definitely headed in the right direction because instead of running away from the problem or saying that shyness is just "who you are" you're actually looking to solve your problem head-on. I congratulate you. This book will definitely help you become more social.

Your success depends on how much time, effort and focus you put into it. Make no mistake about it. To benefit more fully from our social interaction and contribute more value to other people, we need to improve our social skills. This book steps you through a practical success-focus approach to improving your social skills.

Instead of rehashing and recycling the same old psychological stuff and jargon that you get from other social skill builder books, this book instead walks you through several steps which you can take to gain quick results. Please note:

While this book will teach you how to improve your skills in getting along with others, please note that you're not going to go from a complete and total social 0 to a hero overnight.

I need you to get that idea out of your head. This is not one of those heavily hyped "magical" and social transformation books. This book, instead, focuses on practical things you can do on a day to day basis. There's no magic bullet solution. I'm sorry to report that, but that's the absolute truth. Despite what you may have read from other books or the impressions you may have walked away with, overcoming shyness and becoming more social really takes effort. I know that's probably not the kind of message you want to hear, but it's the truth. It's the message that you need to hear.

Accordingly, you need to manage your expectation. The bottom line is you get out what you put in. I don't mean to put a damper on your expectations from this book, but I'd rather set you up for the long, hard road up ahead and condition you for ultimate success rather than to let you down by hyping up quick results.

To reach the height of social mastery, you need to constantly practice, scale up and optimize the information you will learn here. It's important to note that the information I'm going to share with you is just starting point. Feel free to slice and dice them and mix and match them to fit your personality and your set of circumstances.

Still, just by implementing the information I provide you, you'll be in a better position than you are now in terms of getting along with others and making a better impression.

Chapter 1: Get Your Mind Right

Before you begin working on your social skills, your mind must be in the right place. A lot of social skill building books completely dispense with this step. They think that as long as you're pumped up and excited about turning your social skills around and becoming a better people person, that's all that matters.

Unfortunately, it doesn't work that way. Fact is people fail to achieve social skill improvement because they fail to mentally condition themselves. They come in with all sorts of hyped up expectations and a false sense of confidence. They end up hitting a wall. Many of them don't even get around to actually carrying out the things that they've read about.

Don't get me wrong. They're pumped up, motivated and excited, but that's only part of the picture. Time and time again, for whatever reason, these people fail to improve their social skills and they turn around and blame the system. That's right. They blame the books, the life coaches and everybody and anybody except themselves.

Again, I don't mean to be the bearer of bad news here, but it isn't the system that they're using that failed. Instead, they didn't set their mind right. The good news is you don't have to follow their path.

Follow the steps, I'm going to describe below:

Step 1: Believe that the system works

The first thing that you need to do is tap the power of belief. If you don't believe something works, then it's not going to work for you because ultimately, your doubts and skepticism will get the better of you. It's as if you're trying to do something but your doubts keep sabotaging and undermining you. You don't put in as much time, effort and energy as you should. Don't be surprised if things don't pan out like you had hoped.

You may have all sorts of hopes and wishes, but if you, deep down inside, don't really believe that this is going to work out, then don't be shocked if your fears become true. You have to wrap your mind around everything that I will discuss here. Believe that this system works. If it works for other people, it should work for you. There's really no good reason why it shouldn't work.

Step 2: Believe that you can do it

It's one thing to believe that a system will work for other people, but it's another thing entirely to believe that it will work in your personal life. I need you to make that leap of faith. If you already believe that this system works, congratulations.

The next step is to believe that it will work in your situation. Put more simply, believe that you can do it. A lot of people struggle when they read success stories. They get inspired by people starting with pennies ending up billionaires. They get motivated by people who started with nothing or who had to struggle against all sorts of adversity only to come out on top.
The problem is, as motivated and pumped up as they may be, they can't make that leap of faith to apply what they read to their personal lives. The old saying of "If they can do it, you can do it too." doesn't work for them. They cut off the second part of that sentence.

For this step, you have to apply your belief in the system that I'm going to teach you to you. Believe that you yourself can do it. If other people were able to do it, understand that you can do it too. Internalize this fact. Say to yourself, "Yes I can do it. I believe that I can make this system work for myself. I already know it works, but I believe that I can do it. Nobody can do it for me. I have to do it."

Step 3: Believe that it will work in your life

Now that you believe that you can make this system work for you and that you are the person that will make it happen, the next step shouldn't be that big of a leap of faith. The next step is to believe that this system will work in your life. In other words, it would fit whatever is unique, weird, awkward, different in your life.

This is a very important transition because a lot of people put up all sorts of excuses and justifications why a system doesn't work in their particular situation. They know that the system works. They know they're able to make this system work, but they can't make it all the way because they think that their life is too different, too awkward and just too unique.

You have to get rid of this mental clutter and believe that regardless of whatever special arrangements are going on in your life and regardless of your past, your experiences or everything else that is unique about your situation, that the system will still work. Put in another way, your life is not so weird, so different and so out there that this system will not work in your life.

Stop giving yourself excuses. Don't give yourself an out. If you make this leap of faith, then everything will be clearer and more doable. It's not going to be easy because you're going to be overcoming old habits, but at least you see the path ahead of you. But until and unless you go through the 3 steps I mentioned above, you're not going to go far. It doesn't matter how pumped up, motivated or excited you are, you're just not going to make it because these 3 mental hurdles will get you each and every time.

You need to get your mind right otherwise, this book will not help you. In fact, no book will. Sure they may do a great job inspiring you with all sorts of amazing stories and you might even get really motivated because the steps are clear, well explained and pretty straightforward, but unfortunately, intellectual acceptance doesn't translate to actual life changes. Why? Your mind, ultimately, is shut to instruction. You refuse to believe. So get your mind right.

Chapter 2: Get Ready To COMMIT

Getting your mind right is definitely a great first step, but understanding a system and believing that it works and that you would be able to make it work and that it can apply to your life is not going to take you far without one missing ingredient. The ingredient is commitment.

Commitment turns what would otherwise be an idea that stays in your head into something that produces effects in your life. In other words, it changes reality because you stick to it long enough for the idea to change the things you say, the things you think about, and the things you do.

Most people can believe in ideas

As I mentioned above, you can be excited about becoming more social and you can get your mind right. This is due to the fact that most people can believe in the power of ideas. They can see that ideas can solve a problem. Most people can get the need for change. They realize that they need to change. They also can see the tremendous amount of benefits they can get if they implement or carry out some ideas. They understand the problem, they can see the solution and they can see how much better their lives can be. But what's the problem here?

This is all happening in your head. This is all taking place in the form of agreement with certain ideas. Now, this is important and is definitely crucial, but something is missing.

Agreeing to solutions can only take you so far

Since all the realizations described above are happening in your head, it's very tempting to assume that since you mentally agree to these things that this is the same as taking action. I'm sorry, but mentally assenting to something may be important, but you need to develop a sense of emotional urgency. Put in another way, having everything fit together clearly in your mind is not going to take you far unless you take this knowledge and translate it into emotional urgency. In other words, the ideas that you have in your head sinks to the level of your heart so much that you are pushed to take action.

If you just think that your problems are these issues that you kick around in your head and it's just a simple matter of sticking the round peg in the right hole, then everything will be okay. If that's your mindset, you're going to struggle because you're not going to feel the urgency you need to take action.

More importantly, you're not going to feel the emotional urgency to keep taking action. It's not enough to just take action one time. Your life isn't going to change overnight. You have to keep taking action day after day after day. That takes commitment. Commitment ensures that whatever it is that you're excited about in your head sinks to the level of your heart so it changes the things that you say, things that you consistently think about and the actions you constantly take.

Commitment is crucial

When you develop emotional urgency regarding something that you need to do, you will be able to do the following:

You will be able to stick to the plan.

What if I told you that there are going to be bumps in the road? What if I told you that you might face a lot of resistance as you try to become a more social person? The worst part? A lot of this resistance will come from within. I know that sounds crazy, but you yourself will come up with all sorts of excuses to not try as hard or, worse yet, to give up.

Also, you might try to "bargain with yourself" and end up with a compromise that really wears down your social skills over time. Commitment enables you to stick to the plan regardless of how inconvenient or even uncomfortable things get. Regardless of how weird you feel or how awkward you think you are in front of people, you stick to the plan. You put one foot in front of the other and you do it day after day after day.

Commitment enables sacrifice

It's easy for people to focus on what already works. It's easy for people to stick to what is comfortable. Unfortunately, these are precisely the things that you'll need to give up so you can achieve greater victories in life. Becoming more social is one of those things. You're going to have to break out of your comfort zone. I'm sure you'd rather bury your nose in a book or just hang out with one or two close friends and call it a day, but if you really want to achieve a massive breakthrough in your ability to connect to people, you need to push against the walls of your comfort zone. You need to sacrifice the old self and its comfort and conveniences to something completely unknown.

The only way to achieve any breakthrough here is commitment. Commitment enables you to sacrifice. It enables you to override the temptation to just go with the tried and proven and the quick and the easy. Please understand that becoming more social is not an easy thing. You're going to have to override your natural habits. It also takes a lot of time. This sacrifice is not just a one-time thing. It's constant. The only way to make it through this is commitment.

Commitment enables you to do whatever is necessary to achieve progress

Sometimes, you have to think quick on your feet. Sometimes, you need to challenge yourself or put yourself in a really uncomfortable situation to achieve a breakthrough. Now that looks pretty straightforward when you're reading it in a book. It's another thing entirely if you're going to actually carry it out in real life. Doing whatever is necessary sounds awesome when other people are doing it, but when it's your turn, it can get downright scary.

Commitment enables you to overcome your fear. The good news here is the more you do it, the more you get used to it. But you need to make it past that initial stage. This initial stage involves the first or the first three or the first ten times you try to be social within a fairly forbidding and intimidating setting. Commitment enables you to get through this.

Commitment enables you to keep at it regardless of how many times you fail

The difference between successful people and people who are not so successful is not their level of intelligence. You can have two equally intelligent people trying something out and one goes on to success and the other continues to struggle. The big difference really boils down to their ability to handle setbacks.

Since you're going to go against a lot of your existing social instincts as well as your current habits, expect setbacks. Expect things to get really weird. Expect to feel really awkward. In fact, you shouldn't be surprised when you find yourself in a situation where your first impulse is to simply turn around and run away. That's perfectly natural.

Unfortunately, sometimes, you give in to that. You know you failed, but you really can't help it. What do you do in this situation? If you don't commit, it makes it so much easier for you to just continue to fail. You just tell yourself, "I just can't do it. This is not me. This is not who I am."

When you commit to changing yourself, you're going to keep at it regardless of how many times you fail. You may get knocked off, but your commitment enables you to spring back up and you try again and again and again. The good news here is that every single time you get knocked down, you stay on the ground a shorter amount of time. In fact, if you keep this up, you reach a point where you get knocked down, you instantly get back up and eventually, you avoid getting knocked down. For that to happen, you need to commit.

Understand that you will need to commit

Please understand that commitment is not an option. It is an absolute necessity. It's strictly required. If you can't commit, then there's really no point in going further with this book. It's not going to work for you. Unfortunately, no other book will work as well. It's just not going to happen because you can't commit. I need your word right now that you will commit to doing everything listed in this book. Read this book with commitment in mind, otherwise, it's just not going to be able to help you.

Sure you can get pumped up, excited and motivated, but that's not going to be enough. Eventually, that will burn up and you will end up where you began. Commitment is crucial. Are you ready to do it?

Chapter 3: Get Ready To Go On A Journey

Your metaphor for any big life project you do plays a big role in whether you're going to be successful or not. You can look at life as a race, a puzzle or even a prison. Your choice of metaphor sets limits as well as opens opportunities that greatly impact how you experience life. I need you to strongly consider one particular metaphor when it comes to building social skills: A journey

The great thing about journeys is that you don't just go from point A to point B. Instead, the process of getting to your destination changes you because there are many detours, many bumps on the road, many realizations and ideas you run into as you go on with your trip.

Compare this with how most other social skill improvement books position themselves. A lot of them sell themselves as a set of "social hacks" or "social technologies" While there's some value to those metaphors, ultimately, they fall short. Why? Well, hacks are short and shallow solutions. Many "social technologies" are essentially just shortcuts.

While these can help you make some changes, they don't go far enough. What do you need to do? Well, it's actually quite simple. You need to learn how to change how you think about yourself.

Learn to change how you think about yourself

Boosting your social skills effectively means that you have to change certain key elements of yourself. First, you need to learn how to change yourself image. You have a certain image to yourself. You think of yourself in certain terms. In many cases, you might not even be aware of it. You just assume these things.

You need to take a step back, slow down and clearly identify how you describe yourself to yourself. You might be shocked. There might be some surprises there. All this time you have been struggling because of the effect of this self-image that you carry with you. Maybe by being more analytical in getting in touch with who you think you are, you would be able to line up your thoughts, actions and words with yourself image.

Learn how to change your self-esteem

People who are shy often have problems with self-esteem. This is going to be a big issue because if you don't love yourself enough, nobody will do it for you. If you don't respect yourself enough, your performance suffers. You feel that you're less able than other people. If you feel deep down inside that you're really not all that worthy, then don't be surprised about your low self-confidence. It has to come from somewhere.

You have to change your self-esteem and this really all starts with self-acceptance. It's okay not to be perfect. It's okay to not have everything. It's okay to have flaws and be awkward in certain things. Welcome to the club. I got news for you. Everybody else is imperfect. Why should you be any different?

Learn to accept yourself because when you accept yourself, you are no longer imposing impossible standards on yourself which lowers your value in your eyes. Instead, you look at yourself for who you really are. You're the only one who will be able to do this.

Self-esteem leads to self-confidence

Once you have learned to accept yourself more, this can lead to greater and greater self-confidence. Since you understand that you are worth loving and respecting, you're able to take the next leap and assume that you can do things. You can walk into any situation without being afraid that you will screw everything up. After all, in your mind, you are worthy.

Please understand how self-esteem is connected to self-confidence. Get clear on the fact that self-esteem leads to self-confidence. In fact, self-esteem is the bed rock for self-confidence. Not the other way around.

Social skills require self-confidence

Why did we go through the required changes described above? The bottom line is social skills require self-confidence. If you have a lousy self-image, you're going to have a low self-esteem. With low self-esteem, chances are you're going to have very low self-confidence. That's normally how it works. If you don't have enough self-confidence, social interaction is going to be like pulling teeth for you. It's going to be a chore. You'd rather do something else.

It's not hard to figure out why. When you're trying to boost your social skills, you'll be taking risks. You'll be doing things that you don't normally do. You'll be putting yourself in certain situations that you're normally not in. These require self-confidence. Deep down inside, you must feel that you can do it. Otherwise, the risks will seem so heavy that you're tempted to think that it's just not worth it.

You also need self-confidence in building social skills because often times, you'll be operating "out of your element." It would feel like you're a fish out of the water. Without self-confidence, it's easy to let these external pressures of being in a different place in front of different people in a very intimidating environment to just crush you. It just proves to be too much and you just quit.

Finally, social skills enable you to bounce back when you meet with social setbacks. I'm sure you already know that the first time you try anything, chances are good that it won't be smooth. There will be hiccups and you don't end up doing it the right way. You need the self-confidence to bounce back from these situations. It's not a question of if. It's a matter of when because these situations will come up again and again and again.

Understand that all of the above require confidence. You need to find it and you need to use it. Unfortunately, until and unless you learn to change your self-image, which leads to greater self-esteem, you're going to have a harder time. Take care of these foundational issues first before you start working on your social skills.

Chapter 4: Laying The Foundation For Enhanced Social Skills: The Importance Of Self-Confidence

Make no mistake about it. If you want to improve your people skills, you have to operate from a position of strength. You can't just fake it until you make it. For every successful impression you make, you're bound to drop the ball many times over. In fact, you might be sending mixed signals to people. On the one hand, you seem to know what you're doing because you say the right things at the right time to produce the right effects.

However, most of the time, you seem like a fish out of the water. You fumble. You fail to get the message. Non-verbal signals fall between the cracks and you respond negatively. People can't seem to figure out who you are and what you're about.

Without self-confidence, you won't be able to consistently produce the right effect. You won't be able to communicate what you're trying to say because you're operating from a position of weakness. It comes as no surprise that socially inept people often have low self-esteem and self-confidence. These two factors go hand in hand. People who have low self-confidence operate out of fear.

I hope you don't need me to spell out why this is a bad idea. When you are fearful and trying to communicate with people, there's a high likelihood that you're just trying to say stuff that you think they want to hear. You're not really communicating, instead, you're just letting them call the shots and you are trying to walk on egg shells. It really is some sort of elaborate dance because you fear being found out. You fear being judged. You fear being made to feel awkward, weird, abnormal.

Believe it or not, the more you engage in social interactions out of fear, it makes your social skill problems worse. You don't have self-esteem. You don't have self-confidence. You're just taking shots in the dark. You're crossing your fingers and hoping for the best. Last time I checked, that's not exactly a winning strategy.

You can't afford to operate out of fear. Your efforts at building up your social skills must be built on something real. It must be built on the bedrock of self-confidence. Otherwise, you probably are going to get the same results that you're getting now.

Let's get one thing clear here. Nobody is a complete and total social loser, okay? Let's get that out of the way. Even if you think you are the most socially inept person on the face of the planet, chances are you have some friends. Chances are there are some people who have a favorable impression of you. You haven't completely dropped the ball. You're not a social disaster across the board.

The reason for this, of course, is the fact that from time to time, you do manage to create a positive social connection. Everybody's capable of this. But if you truly want to enhance your social skills so you can consistently produce positive social interaction, you need to step out of this. You need to get out of the shadow of a random chance because that's what all this is. That's all you have.

Some days are better than others, but you don't really know when the next good day is going to come around. That, unfortunately, is not a winning strategy. It never was, it isn't now, and it probably will never be a winning strategy. You have to have something more consistent, predictable and stable.

The reason for this erratic results is due to the fact you often suffer from a social downward spiral. It works out in roughly this way. You have low self-esteem. Deep down, at some level or other, you feel you're not worthy. You might even think you're an impostor, a fraud, or somebody who's just trying to pass himself or herself off as somebody they're not.

Whatever the case may be, you think you are not good enough. This, of course, is not a good foundation for self-confidence. At some level or other, you feel you're just not capable. You may psyche yourself up to try, but it isn't good enough. You just don't have that level of confidence. You don't feel like whatever it is that you're about to do has a high likelihood of success. This leads to you second-guessing yourself.

This leads to you misreading the social signals being sent to you. Time and time again, this leads to bad or awkward social attempts. Your efforts at reaching out and trying to make other people comfortable and otherwise, engage in a two-way discussion is not as good as it could be. In fact, in many cases, it ends up in failure. You feel awkward, weird, the person is put off or even offended. What do you think happens when that plays out? It leads to lower self-esteem on your part. You get direct evidence, at least that's how you're reading this, that you are not worthy. That there is something wrong with you. There is something missing.

This lower self-esteem corrodes your willingness to try again. You're thinking to yourself, "Well, the last time I tried to reach out ended up in failure. It was a mess. I probably won't try that again." Well, just like with anything else in life, the less you do something, the worse you get at it. Make no mistake about it. Even the most proficient, prolific and skilled salespeople started out as bumbling idiots. They can't make a pitch, they talk over themselves, they can't make eye contact or they rush through things because they're so eager to make the sale and it all ends up at the same place. People fall flat on their face and make a complete and total fool of themselves, but they try again, and again, and again.

In the beginning, it's almost 100% failure rate. That's right. 100% failure rate. But as they get up and try again, they try to connect the dots and do something a little bit different. They focus on what works and build on that. They pay attention to areas for improvement and work around those. Sooner or later, they are able to hit their stride. They succeed again, and again, and again.

I wish I could tell you that this all happens overnight. I wish I could tell you that all of this will automatically take place the moment you try. It doesn't work that way. Life is not like that. You have to try and unfortunately, when you're caught in this social downwards spiral, your lower self-esteem and lower estimation of your worth makes it less likely for you to try. This means that you're not putting yourself in a position to get better at social interaction. What do you think happens?

Just like refusing to go the gym, your social muscles start to get weaker and weaker. This leads to worse social skills. At certain situations, you have to get out there. You have to talk to strangers. You have to try to make a connection. What do you think happens? Remember, you did not give yourself enough practice. That's right. You fail. So the process repeats itself again. You interpret things in the worst way possible and you say to yourself, "Maybe I am a complete and total social loser."

And the process repeats itself over and over again and you go down this downwards spiral until you have pretty much nothing left.

You have to understand that you need the self-confidence to get out from under all of this, but for self-confidence to appear, you have to build self-esteem. Pay attention to that phrase "self-esteem" In other words, it's your estimation of who you are, what you're about and what your value is. Nobody can give it to you. This is an affirmative decision on your part. You have to call the shots. Are you worthy or not?

From there, self-confidence arises and armed with self-confidence, you can interact socially better. Understand how these different factors flow into each other. You can't build great social skills on the sand. You can't just assume a role. You can't just look at a script and act a part. It doesn't work that way. You will be found out. People will think you are a fake. Worst of all, you will think you're the biggest impostor on the planet. Don't even get started on that road. Instead, focus on building on something real.

Chapter 5: Improve Your Self-Esteem By Learning To Love Yourself

Now that you have decided that you are going to build your self-confidence on the real bedrock of self-esteem, just how exactly are you going to go about doing that?

There are lots of self-esteem books out there and if you were to really distill them into the simplest truth, it really all boils down to self-love. I know that sounds selfish. To some people, that might even sound rude and self-seeking, but hey, let's get real here. Nobody can love you like yourself.

I know you probably at least have one person telling you that you mean everything to them, they can't live without you, that you complete them etc. etc. But let me tell you, when the chips are down, they still have to take care of themselves. There is such a thing called self-preservation. They have to take care of themselves so they can take care of the others. This means that nobody can love you like yourself. You have to take the initiative. You can't wait for somebody else to give you the love that you deny yourself.

The bottom line is everybody's got their own issues. People have enough problems of their own. They have lives to take care of. While they can care tremendously about you and go a long way in helping you, the bottom line is nobody can love you like yourself. It is an affirmative decision on your part. Nobody can step in and give you the love you deserve. You are going to have to do that. The question then becomes, are you even worth loving in the first place?

Let's get real here. I know this hurts. I know this is awkward. This is probably a question you'd rather avoid, but you need to face it straight on, otherwise, you're not going to achieve any kind of progress. Are you worth loving? And the answer better be yes. I don't care what your past is. I don't care what you've done. I don't care how ugly you think you are. I don't care inept you think you are at sports, at school, at work. There's something about you that is lovable.

Unfortunately, the only person who is equipped to find out is yourself. The only person who's in the best position to find out is you. There's something about you that is lovable. Are you willing to find it? Are you willing to search for it?

I'm not talking about potential here because hey, let's get real again, everybody can talk a big game about potential. I can potentially be the next governor of my state. Everybody's got that potential if you think about it hard enough. Given enough time, effort, energy and focus, there are few things off limits to the typical human being.

The sad reality is that whatever limitation that we are working with are chosen limitations. I know it doesn't seem like it. The lack of money at the end of the month, the rent that's coming due, the impossible mortgage payments. But if you really are completely honest with yourself, these are non-issues. If you really believed in your potential, these are not issues. You can find a way.

This is the realm of potential. I'm talking about something that already exists. I'm talking about something about you that is lovable which is not theoretical, speculative or philosophical. It already exists. What is it?

Maybe it's some sort of skill. Maybe you like to sing. Maybe you like to rhyme. Maybe you have a weird sense of humor that you make all sorts of weird puns or you try to pair different ideas together. Maybe you have a very interesting talent like you're able to dictate from just one word or sentence a whole book. Maybe you are able to look at patterns when you look at a painting in such a way that escapes most people. Maybe you even have a very interesting laugh. Perhaps you have a habit that you always fall into that you can't shake that people admire. Personally, I admire people who are able to wake up at 2 am every single day regardless of how tired they are the previous night. Maybe you have some sort of instinct that you are able to read people despite knowing absolutely nothing about them. Maybe you have some sort of sixth sense regarding situations and it always proves to be correct. Or it may be something else.

But I need you to pay attention to everything that I've said prior to this point. I want it to be clear that what makes you lovable does not lie outside of you. Believe it or not, it has nothing to do with your physical appearance. You might have beautiful, shiny, blonde or platinum hair and deep, gorgeous green eyes, but physical appearance can change. You may have this youthful luster to you, this amazing glow that makes you so beautiful, but hey, people gain weight, they develop wrinkles over time, they change. That's part of life. We are all encased in flesh. Last time I checked flesh, the human body and the human image are not immune to time.

What makes you lovable is locked within you. These are things that won't change unless you want them to. These are attributes that can't be easily taken away.

I want you to zero in on the things that make you different. Try to write them down. Be completely honest with yourself. One way to do this is to just simply jump in with both feet and say to yourself point blank, "What makes me weird? What makes me abnormal? What makes me strange?" Write it down. You'd be surprised as to how beautiful, interesting, intriguing and engaging you can be.

You have to understand that for the most part, people fear the weird, abnormal, unusual, strange and awkward aspect of their personality. They try to run away from it, and most importantly, they try to hide it from everybody else.

What if I told you that you should be doing the complete 180 degrees opposite? What if I told you that you should not fear the weird, instead, this is what makes you so interesting. You have to understand that when you fall in love with somebody, they're not going to say to you "Oh I'm falling in love with you because you're just like that guy/woman that I liked before." They would tell you that they love you because you have traits that are special. It's unique to you and they can't help but fall in love with that. In other words, they're falling in love with your flaws, imperfections, blemishes, and these are internal blemishes mind you. Most of the time, they're just in your head.

People who truly love you, whether in the form of lovers or friends, focus on what's different. They focus on what's weird, abnormal, quirky, in fact, one of my best friends in college was drawn to the fact that I had a tough time saying the word "three" clearly. Instead it would come off as "tree" as in the plant. It was only one day after we had some beers that I learned that that's what drew his attention to me.

That's how you make friends. They're not drawn by how perfect you are. They're not attracted by how well you fit some sort of universal standard that applies to all people at all times and in all cultures. They're not looking for a trait of yours that everyone has. If you think about it, it makes all the sense in the world. If you are attracted to somebody who has a trait that everybody else has, then why are you attracted to that person? You see how this works?

Unfortunately, a lot of people with low self-esteem focus on what they're missing. They feel that they have to apologize for something. They feel that they're really not complete until they're like everybody else. Well, flip the script because this is the absolute truth. People love you because you're weird, different, missing something, awkward. This is not something to apologize for.

Embrace your oddity

Everyone's odd. Get that through your thick skull. Seriously. No joke. Real story. People might play a good game hiding this fact, but it's not going to go away. Everybody's odd. Yeah, that's right. Everybody's strange, there's something weird about them, that's what makes us lovable and distinct. That's what draws people to us and I'm talking about real friends here. I'm not talking about people who are drawn to you because you add social cache or value to them. There are those kinds of friends. Let's get real here.

I'm talking about real friends. These are people who'd die for you. People who'd sacrifice everything because your friendship means so much to them and guess what, they love you because you're different. They love you because you're odd. Accept and embrace these things about yourself. There's nothing to explain. You don't have to make excuses for these. Just assume that this is lovable.

I'm not talking about stuff that you do that makes you feel guilty. Like if you have this "unusual habit" of killing homeless people on the weekends, that's not what I'm talking about. That's a joke, but I hope you get the point. I'm talking about things that you normally feel awkward about. Embrace these. By embracing them, you no longer have to make them operate in such a way that they corrode your self-esteem. They don't make you less of a person.

Chapter 6: Self-Acceptance Leads To Greater Self-Esteem

Now that you have embraced your oddity, congratulations. You are definitely several steps away to fully accepting yourself. Self-acceptance is crucial to a healthy self-esteem. You will never find yourself worthy, capable or good enough if you don't accept yourself. Learn to fully accept.

I'm not talking about mental acceptance here because, hey, let's face it, everybody can do that. If you go to a high school lecture room, you can accept all sorts of stuff that the teacher throws your way. That's not the kind of acceptance I'm talking about. I'm talking about accepting these with your heart because once we hear stuff and it enters our minds and we intellectually become comfortable with information, we then end up incorporating it. But this isn't good enough.

You have to incorporate it so much that it changes how you feel about things. It has to have some sort of emotional effect. This is how you learn to accept yourself fully. This is how you learn to love different parts of yourself. You have to remember that most people love certain parts of themselves but hate everything else. While they can function, they can't function fully because there are certain parts that are off limits. They end up sabotaging and undermining themselves as they try to break out of these limitations, but they can't. How can you? It's like trying to box Floyd Mayweather with one hand tied behind your back. Good luck with that.

Practice affirmations

I wish I could tell you that self-acceptance is pretty straightforward and basic and just needs some sort of intellectual exercise. Unfortunately, it doesn't work that way. You have to be proactive and take matters into your own hands. You have to take initiative and one of those ways to do this is to practice affirmations.

As you probably already know, affirmations are viewed by mass media and our general culture as something cheesy. The first image that comes to mind is somebody looking in the mirror and saying to themselves "You are good enough. You're a champion. I believe in you." Well, that's the Hollywood image of affirmations, but you need to go beyond the stereotype because there's a lot of truth to affirmations.

What if I told you you're already practicing affirmations but it often trips you up? That's right. You're engaged in some sort of daily affirmation practice that throws you off track. There is such a thing as self-talk. This is an inaudible soundtrack that you play in your mind. You're saying things about yourself. You're making judgments about yourself. But this plays on auto-pilot at the back of your mind. It starts to play automatically in certain situations.

The reason why people don't have a tremendous amount of self-acceptance is that they are playing the wrong soundtrack. Try it. Be more mindful of this script that you are reciting to yourself. You'd be surprised at the things that you say about yourself, your capabilities, your place in the world and what you're about. For example, if you stub your toe, the first thing that comes to your mind is "I'm an idiot." or "I'm dumb." or if your boss tells you that you're not going to get that raise, it's not uncommon for people to play a soundtrack that says in so many words "I'm a loser."

When you play these things, whether you're aware of them or not, they do have an impact because you're constantly programming your reality. Your mind and body are always listening to this and if you keep saying the same things over and over again, what do you think will happen? You're having problems accepting yourself because chances are, you are playing the wrong script.

Practicing affirmations is simply a conscious way of reversing whatever negative programming you are automatically playing in certain situations. You are fully conscious of you speaking some sort of reality into your life. When you look into the mirror and you say "I'm smart enough. I can do this. I've done this before." And then you spell out the scenarios where certain traits of your paid off.

You're not doing this to hypnotize yourself. You're not engaged in some sort of self-delusion, instead, this is based on facts. Because, let me tell you, regardless of how hard that project you're struggling with, you've done something similar to it in the past. It might be at a low level, but you've done something similar enough. So by focusing on those and the fact that you were able to achieve something positive, you can say to yourself with a straight face and with all honesty, "I can do this."

For example, if my project is to travel 10,000 miles, I only need to look at the fact that in the past, I've traveled 3,000 miles. So I say to myself, "I've done this before. I can do this. I have it in me." Do you see the difference between this line of affirmation and the script that people normally say to themselves? They say, "This is completely new. It's going to be difficult. There's going to be many problems up ahead and you will not have a clue because this is so new." Focus on the facts because big goals that seem so intimidating and so huge and monstrous can be broken down into small parts.

A lot of those small parts actually relate to things that you have done in the past. Think of it as something like building a pyramid with small bricks. You've done bricks in the past, so as intimidating and as scary as a huge pyramid may seem, when you look at the small pieces, you can't help but feel comforted.

You can't help but feel this is not all that unfamiliar. Do you see where I'm coming from here?

Practice affirmations. It's not cheesy. It's not a waste of time. Instead, it's an exercise of personal power over your immediate reality. The reason why you're continuing to struggle and feel frustrated is because you're playing the wrong soundtrack. Isn't it high time that you consciously switch that off and try something that you can control?

Practice self-worth inventory

At the same time, you're practicing affirmations, I also need you to do a self-worth inventory. This has nothing to do with bragging. A lot of us grew up in households where bragging or any other kind of attention seeking was looked down upon. I guess you can say that parents wanted the very best for us so they wanted to spare us from the potential misunderstandings that could arise when we draw too much attention to ourselves or alternatively, they're correct for not wanting us to become braggers. These are people who talk a good game but always under deliver. These people who talk big but can never walk their talk. It's okay for parents to not want their children to develop into those people, but often times, they go overboard. They end up suppressing their children's natural tendency to talk about their achievements and their successes.

If you come from a household where your parents went overboard and basically dismissed any kind of self-congratulation as empty pride or being boastful, this exercise will help you tremendously. I need you to do a self-worth inventory.

On a sheet of paper, in all honesty, list any and all achievements. It doesn't have to be big. It doesn't have to be grandiose. It doesn't have to involve you showing up at a Nobel prize award ceremony. Any kind of award or achievement will do. Similarly, write down any kind of skill you have.

Now here's the thing about skills. As long as it's not readily available in a generalized form, it is a skill. For example, if you can sing and carry a tune, that's a skill because most people can't carry a tune well enough. It would even be better if you won some sort of contest because that would provide objective validation to your skill level.

If you know how to argue in front of a lot of people and win debates, that's a great skill. If you know how to speak off the cuff when somebody gives you one sentence or five words and you are able to think up of a novel or a short story or a self-help book or even a long drawn out poem from it. That's a skill. Dig deep. Don't be shy. This is no time to hold back. Again, you're not dealing with your parents who quickly told you to stop bragging. This is the time to rise and shine as far as your skills, accomplishments, achievements and everything else positive are concerned.

Also, write down happy memories. One of my happiest memories is when I taught my son how to pray. I also taught him how to recite poetry. Focus on happy memories. These are things that give you pride, help you feel like you've done something positive. It doesn't have to be big. It doesn't have to be grandiose where people have to hang a medal on your neck for doing it. Instead, it just has to burn deeply in your heart. That's how positive it is.

Next, list down great praises you have gotten from other people. For example, somebody said to you, "You are a very smart person." or "You are very clever." As much as possible, list down stuff that has nothing to do with external characteristics. As much as possible, leave off the list complements about your looks because hey, let's face it, looks fade. Focus on these praises.

Give yourself enough time to compile a massive self-worth inventory. This is your time. This is a celebration of everything and anything great about you. Anything that's noteworthy and positive, list it down. Knock yourself out.

Remember this

After you've listed down everything, I need you to filter it. I want you to look at what your achievements mean. I want you to look at your skills and also other people's praise of you and what internal realities they point to. What do these things mean? What is it about you that is special that you can wrap your mind around. In other words, distill or filter the initial list that you have.

The end result of this should be a list of traits that are purely internal and are not worth on other people's assessment. Don't get me wrong, they may be able to provide objective validation, but it really all boils down to you possessing these traits internally. You have to actually recognize these traits. Can you really see it? Is it real enough to you? Then that's good enough because you should not base yourself worth on what other people say or think.

Think about it this way, if you're going to live your life based on other people's approval, what will happen when that approval disappears? It will dry up like the morning dew. What's left? Do you see where I'm coming from?

Focus instead on what all this external validation is pointing to. Base it on your own worth. Base it on your evaluation of what these things mean. You must have value to yourself. Why? Only you can give yourself value. This takes quite a bit of time because let's face it, we're social animals. For the longest time, we have let other people define us. We have let our need for social approval and external validation shape our ego and our self-esteem.

Now you're flipping the script. You're now focusing on the value you give yourself. Understand that this is an exercise of control and willpower. It is a choice. Don't ever forget that. So go through this process. Maybe it will take you a whole day. Maybe it will take you several days. Regardless of how long it takes, do it. It's definitely going to be one of the most important things you will ever do because if you do this right, you will have a foundation for self-confidence and once you have this foundation set properly, everything else becomes possible as far as enhancing your social skills are concerned.

You need to set this base and unfortunately, it can be uncomfortable. You might be drawing a blank right now. You might be thinking to yourself, "Well, if I strip out all external validation and what other people tell me, then I'm left with nothing." Well, that's going to be a problem. Focus instead on what these external points refer to. They're not wasting their time. They're not seeing things that aren't there. Dig deep. Look at their frame of reference. What are they referring to? At least it's real enough. Focus on that.

Chapter 7: What is Self-Confidence Anyway?

Before we jump into an exploration of the connection between self-confidence and improved social skills, we need to focus on defining self-confidence. As I mentioned in the previous chapters, if you do not have a healthy self-esteem, you won't be confident in yourself. This doesn't mean that you can't appear confident. This does not mean that you can't fake it until you make it.

However, as I have mentioned previously, you're probably going to get very spotty results. You're not going to get the kind of consistent results people are looking for. People might think you're fake. People might think that you are very selective or there's just something wrong with how you interact with people because it's not even, it's not consistent, it's not smooth.

This can be traced to the fact that you don't have the self-esteem needed to produce the kind of self-confidence required for smooth, consistent and effective social skills. That's how important self-confidence is but a crucial component to this is a clear working definition of what self-confidence is and what it isn't.

Self-confidence is not self-esteem. A lot of people think they're one and the same. They're not.

Self-esteem focuses on whether you think you're worthy. It involves your valuation of who you are, what you're about and what you can contribute to the rest of the world. It says volumes about what you think your place is in the world.

Self-confidence, on the other hand, is an impression of trust in your abilities, you're traits, your qualities as a person and your ability to judge things. In other words, it measures how comfortable you are in making decisions in the world around you. You're always making decisions. You're always sizing things up. You're always trying to figure things out. Self-confident people are able to trust themselves to do the right thing at the right time to produce the right results with the right people.

People who like self-confidence may be able to do things properly. It's not a question of proficiency or competence. They may know how to do things the right way at the right time with the right tools with the right people to produce the great effects. That's not the problem. The problem is they do not trust their ability to achieve a certain outcome. Do you see the difference?

Unfortunately, if you don't have a healthy self-esteem, you are going to distrust yourself. You're going to consistently second-guess yourself. You may hesitate quite a bit. In fact, in many cases, you might be afraid of what you can do.

I'm not saying that you're fearful that you will be able to do things. Instead, it's the precise opposite. You're afraid that you might screw things up. You're afraid that somehow some way, you'll step on people toes, offend people or otherwise make a fool out of yourself.

Again, this has nothing to do with your ability to do things the right way. This has nothing to do with your knowledge levels, your skills, your competency or your proficiency. You might actually be very, very competent, but the problem is you do not trust yourself enough because of low self-esteem. You fear yourself. You fear the consequences.

Self-confidence is all about stepping past that fear. You no longer have to fear yourself because you can trust that when you make that call, it will work out for the best. It's not a one-time thing. This is not a fluke. It happens all the time because you trust yourself enough. It all boils down to being confident in what you can do.

Unfortunately, there are many myths out there that trip people up all the time when it comes to self-confidence. They don't know that they believe in these myths, but these come up again and again, and the results are all too predictable. People run out of steam. They get butterflies in the stomach.

Instead of getting out there, taking a risk, flexing those social muscles, they pull back. It's not because they do not know the right thing to say. It's not because they're not properly equipped. They just don't trust themselves.

These myths erode your trust in yourself. Be aware of them. Understand how they work. Understand their effects.

Myth #1: You have to be the very best in some activity for you to be confident in it

This is one of the most popular lies people tell themselves about self-confidence. Basically, it's an excuse. Seriously.

You know you're good at something, but you also know that you're not the very best in it. You're not exactly in the global top ten as far as singing, dancing, improvisational speaking, public speaking or working at certain jobs are concerned.

However, it shouldn't matter. You're just giving yourself an excuse. You're giving yourself an out so you don't have to try as hard.

The truth is you don't have to be the very best. Far from it. You just need to do it well enough. This is the key. You have to be able to do it "well enough." Understand that defining this phrase boils down to your situation. It changes from situation to situation.

For example, you may think that your singing voice is so bad that you will wake the dead. You're not very confident, to say the least. What if you were in a group of friends and they turned out to be worse singers than you. We're talking about people whose singing voices are like the scratching sound that you hear when you hear somebody scratching a blackboard. In that particular situation, you sound like the next coming of Christine Aguilera or Justin Timberlake.

Do you understand how this works? Do you see it? It's situational. It's comparative.

Please understand that since your ability is situational, then it's good enough because if it's worthwhile in a particular context, then it would work in other contexts. It may not be the very best in the world, but that's okay. You don't have to be a hero.

The key here is to gain a sense of possibility, control or a sense that you can make things happen with that ability. Even if you don't do something exceptionally well, that's good enough because you can always scale it up later. It's more important to gain that sense of trust that this skill that I have, this personal quality that I have, my ability to judge things, it's not the worst. It actually works, and that is good enough. You can scale it up later. You can polish it at some future point in time.

Myth #2: Real confidence is objective

This trips up a lot of people. They think that for confidence to be real enough for them to trust, it must be validated first by other people. Wrong. While it's important to have some sort of external validation, it doesn't have to be much.

For example, you love singing in the shower, and if just one person says, "You love to sing and you sound good," that's good enough. You don't have to be the top contestant at American Idol to feel confident about your singing abilities.

As long as it's based on just a very low-level or even singular objective assessment, that's okay because ultimately confidence can only come from you. You're the one judge whose vote counts the most. Everything else really doesn't matter.

It really all boils down to your read of any situation or your interpretation of what happened. That's where your confidence is going to come from, and that's where the trust is going to arise. It's much better to just go with that feeling and take more action and keep at it.

I remember the first time I went on dates during college. I would approach women, and I would get shot down a lot. However, from time to time, women would smile at me and then they would complement me and I would complement them back, and it would go to a certain to a certain place and then it would fall apart.

Nonetheless, that was good enough for me. I had something to hang my head on, so to speak. I wasn't this complete and total disaster as far as dating was concerned. It's not like women get a glimpse of my image and then they turn around running and shaking. It's not like I was the hunchback of Notre Dame.

The fact that there was some positivity there was good enough for me to go with that feeling. So, I went the weekend after weekend and sometimes on Wednesday nights and I'm happy to report that I had quite a bit of success, and it doesn't matter whether the woman was the redhead, blond, brunette. It doesn't matter which part of the country or the world she came from.

I was able to become confident because I allowed myself to get rid of my dependence on a need for a tremendous amount of objective validation. A few kind words here and there, that's good enough for me. A few smiles from really attractive women every once in a while, that was good enough for me.

Now, somebody else operating with those set of facts probably would have a much tougher time because they would want a lot of women to pay attention to them the moment they step into the club or to the bar. That's going to be a problem because that's usually not how things work out. What happens when you cannot get that objective validation? Where's your confidence now?

So, go with that feeling, and here is the clincher. Take action and keep taking action and, eventually, the victories will start piling up. They would start to outnumber the awkward moments. They would start to exceed the times when you fell flat on your face.

Nobody can do this for you. You have to decide to do this. It's not going to be easy. It can be murder on your ego, but you need to do it because confidence can only come from you.

Myth #3: Self-Confidence is all in your head

Make no mistake about it while it is subjective, and only you can give it yourself, it does have an objective effect. This is how it works out. When you allow yourself to be self-confident, it will have a positive effect on people around you.

Going back to my dating example. A lot of the women in my graduate school class who used to give me the cold shoulder started paying more attention to me because I started becoming more successful with other women.

Don't get me wrong. It's not because they're like keeping tabs on each other. It's not like there's some sort of social network saying, "Oh, okay, this person's sexual stock is going up, so let me see what's up." No, I'm not talking about that.

Instead, they can sense in the way I walked, the way I dressed, the way I talked to people, the way I looked at people's eyes that there was something different. This is the objective effect that I'm talking about because self-confidence starts out as a subjective trust in your abilities to get things done or to produce a certain effect with people.

However, there is an objective effect because there is a "call and response" effect. The more confident you are inside, the more confident you appear to other people. They then send you signals or feedback affirming your confidence, so you become even more confident. This is the objective effect that I'm talking about. When this happens, you're able to handle more and more setbacks.

Have you ever noticed that the really confident friends of yours can tell a joke, bomb and make a complete ass of themselves, brush themselves off and try another joke and over and over it goes until they kill the crowd and everybody laughs? That's how confident people handle themselves.

You can do the same because the more confident you are, the more setbacks you will be able to handle. If you're not a very confident person, and you are operating from a position of really low self-esteem, even the slightest rejection is enough to devastate you.

When you project confidence, it has an objective effect, and it enables you to handle setbacks better. You try and try, and you keep scaling up and you keep fine-tuning. It's not like you keep throwing out the same lines when you are on Tinder or when you are out dating.

You experiment, you connect the dots and you figure out quickly what works and what doesn't. You build on your strengths, you achieve more success and you become more and more confident.

Here's the truth

Here's the truth about self-confidence. It is built on competence. I know you're probably scratching your head because you've read earlier that self-confidence does not depend on your competence. Well, the key here is that competence does not necessarily equate to self-confidence. Just because you know how to do something doesn't mean that you trust yourself to do it the right way each time. You have to go through a specific stage.

You have to look at your competence and accept it. You're going to stop apologizing for it. You're going to say, "This is part of who I am" and tying that into your increased self-esteem, you would then be able to build on it.

However, just working by itself, competence is not going to help you all that much because you don't trust yourself enough. Do you see how this works? Real self-confidence is built on competence, but they are not one and the same. They are not replacements of each other.

Take an assessment of your traits and skills

How do you build self-confidence? Well, I already stepped you through an exercise earlier to help you build self-esteem. The next step is to build self-confidence. You have to accept yourself. You have feel good about yourself. You have to embrace yourself first. That's important. You must do this with the assumption that you are worthy, that you are worth loving, that you are worth liking, the whole nine yards.

With that out of the way, take an assessment of your traits and skills. Just write down what your traits are and the things that you do. Now that you have listed everything down, focus on one. Pick one. Which skill do you think you like the most? Which skill do you think really says a lot about you and what you're about and who you think you are?

Get good enough with at least one skill

The key here is to zero in on a skill and get good enough on it. This might mean you have to brush up on it. This might mean that you have to try it over and over again to get better at it. Whatever the case may be you start using this ask your confidence base because at the back of your head, you are so competent in it that you can trust it fully.

Remember competence, in of itself, is not going to make you self-confident. You have to trust, and to unlock this trust, you must invest enough time, focus and energy on that skill to make it look good enough in your eyes.

This is the base of your confidence and your self-worth because you know, in objective terms, you're competent. Nobody can take that away from you. You've worked on it. You can see it. You can measure it. You feel good about it and, ultimately, you trust it.

Adopt the right ritual

This is a mental ritual that I use when I'm going to be engaging in any kind of activity that requires self-confidence. For example, if I'm going to be speaking in front of a large group of people and I've only been handed a script at the last minute, I used this ritual. This way, I can speak extemporaneously, and the words that come out of my mouth actually make sense to human beings.

It's not exactly easy. I use this ritual so I don't get butterflies in the stomach and eat my words. When I first started doing improvisational speaking in front of random strangers. I end up eating my words. I didn't fully trust my train of thought. I wasn't really all that confident in my ability to clearly express these thoughts in a logical, orderly manner.

Moreover, I was not quite sure of my emotional vocabulary and so I wasn't exactly picking the right words that made the right emotional impact. However, once I started adopting this ritual, things started to click. I wish I could tell you that it was smooth right out of the gate. It wasn't. There were a lot of stumbles, thrills, chills, and spills along the way but, eventually, things worked out.

The same applies to you. I understand it's going to be rough at first because you're used to basically crawling into your shell and just letting things pass by. However, you can't do that anymore.

For you to be self-confident, you have to get out of your shell. You have to try and try and try. This means sometimes you scrape your knee. Sometimes you fall on your ass. That's part of the game. You need to get back up and oftentimes you just need the right ritual.

How do I do it? Well, use this is a framework. What I mean by that is use this as a starting point. Feel free to customize it, slice and dice it, mix and match and otherwise make it fit your particular set of personal circumstances or experience. However, you need to use some sort of ritual.

So, what I do? I look out in front of me and there's a sea of unfamiliar faces. A lot of people are looking at their watches. They're obviously stressed but. Obviously, many, based on the appearance on their faces, do not want to be there.

There I am with this scrap of paper with maybe four words, and I'm supposed to deliver a twenty- to thirty-minute speech. Here's what I do.

First, I start with my competence. I know that I can speak extemporaneously. How do I know that? Because I've spoken in front of strangers before. I haven't been lynched. People haven't run me out of town with pitchforks and torches. So, I guess that's a good thing.

Furthermore, l have made people laugh. I have made people cheer. People have put their hands together and clapped. I have based these on facts so I know that I am competent. Thus, I start there.

Certain mental images come to mind. As I pan through the crowd, checking out different people from different walks of life, wearing different outfits, all these past images flash through my mind. These are images of success. These are images of me demonstrating my competence.

I started to chill at this point because I've been here before this is not completely virgin territory. I'm not exactly a fish out of the water. I've done this before.

After I do that, I then mentally focus on my self-worth. Am I worthy? Am I good enough? Am I worth something? The answer obviously is yes because people like me. I have friends. I have a son who loves me and whom I adore. He's everything to me. I have a wife who understands me and loves me, and I prize her.

Focus on your self-worth. What are you worthy? Why are you worthy? I like helping people. I contributing knowledge or researching and then sharing that knowledge. I like inspiring people.

So, I go through this routine of why are you worthy? Please understand that this flows from competence because I'm trying to build trust here, and I won't feel it unless I lay down the competence first. So, it goes from there and then I go through my self-esteem and self-worth. Basically, based on what I know about myself, what I've done and what I know I'm capable of, worthy. I'm good enough. I can do well here and anywhere.

So, I say this myself really quickly. I scan the room with a smile on my face and certain calm and relaxation overcome me. I slowly yet firmly stick my chest out. I'm no longer slouched. I'm no longer avoiding eye contact. I look around, and I see these people have come to me, hear me. I'm worth listening to at least for the first few minutes.

I go through those scenes and this is enough to pump up my confidence. I've done this before. I can do it again. I've done this in a small way and now I'm in front of a crowd that's larger, I can do it again. If I can do it at a lower level, I can do it at a higher level too.

You have to think along these lines. You have to pump yourself up. Whether we're talking about scale, duration, quality, you have to pump up your confidence.

Next, I practice affirmations. Again, this happens very quickly because it's all in your head, and you do this with a smile on your face, and you look relaxed and chill. I say to myself, "You're good enough. These people came to listen to you. You can speak better than many of these people. You know the subject matter better than these people and you're here to help them. You're here to add value to their lives. Your life has a purpose. There's meaning to this activity.

Then I think back to memories involving meaning. I think back to the feeling I got when people first clapped or that one time when I won an award in high school that's how I get into the zone. That's how I pump myself up because once you're in the zone, own and you start doing your thing, you enter into a state of flow. It's like one right after the other. It's kind of like putting one foot in front of the other.

I remember one time when I was a member of a business group and we had to make this presentation in front of a notoriously difficult investor. We needed this guy's money; otherwise, the company would probably go belly up. That's how crucial this meeting was. Sure enough, we go to this boardroom in Arizona and this really distinguished gentleman showed up. However, he was the stereotypical older gentleman with a tremendous amount of money with that classic no-nonsense look. He didn't even shake my hand.

To make a long story short, the two guys who he shook hands with heartily and who he liked a lot because they fit a certain profile fell flat on their faces. They could not answer his questions. So, he was frustrated, and he said, "Can anybody answer this question?," and I said, "Yes, you are absolutely correct" and I made projections for him. I did the math in my head and, most importantly, I tied it into real-life scenarios that impacted profit and loss.

In other words, I answered the question the way he wanted it answered and with no BS, no evasions, no excuses, no justifications. I laid out the gold along with the garbage because there is a lot of garbage. There are a lot of risks. There is a tremendous amount of reward but, yes, there are rough spots. I did not smooth anything out. I didn't paint d a nice, rosy picture, and he respected that.

At the end of that meeting, he shook my hand so hard that I thought he was going to yank my arm off, and he barely noticed the other dudes I was with. I earned his respect.

I could not have done that if I did not get into the zone because when you get into that flow, no matter how intimidating the people are around you, no matter how high the stakes are, you are able to focus. You're able to zero in on the trust you have in your ability. It all flows out.

This doesn't just apply to business meetings. It applies to meeting members of the opposite sex. Believe me, I've met really attractive women. I mean, they're just so attractive and so stunning that you lose control of your faculties.

It's as if you're watching a movie. They're that stunning. We're talking way beyond the model material. That's saying a lot because I used to live in Los Angeles and, as you know, there are a lot of actresses and models there so the standard is pretty high.

This also applies to school. You can be in graduate school and part of the curriculum is question-and-answer sessions involving the Socratic method. Talk about intellectual torture. A lot of this stuff is not even in the syllabus. In fact, a lot of people say that the Socratic method, whether it's in MBA school or law school or any other high-level graduate program, is a legalized form of intellectual, academic and personal torture.

I can see where people are coming from because, hey, it's like being stripped naked in front of other people. These are your peers. These are people whose respect you're trying to earn and, suddenly, you fall flat on your face in a very public way because you don't know the answer. It's one thing to not know the answer in a private situation, but the professor will make it very public. It's as if there is this giant spotlight in front of you and you're wearing this Ronald McDonald's outfit, a complete and total clown.

Regardless of the situation, the ritual I described above will work for you. Again, you can customize, you can plug and play a bit, you can mix and match. However, as long as you have a ritual, you can get into the zone because it starts to flow, and the great thing about this? The more you get into the zone, the more you flow, the more confident you become about your abilities and, most importantly, the more you love and accept yourself.

Your self-esteem rises. Your self-confidence increases and this can be objectively verified because of your demeanor changes.

You perform differently. You have a higher standard. You're able to hit higher thresholds of quality. It's all internal. Nobody can take this away from you.

Start the ritual today and challenge yourself every single day.

<u>I have another good book for you on Self-Confidence.</u>

Self Confidence: Unleash Your Hidden Potential and Breakthrough Your Limitations of Confidence
(Available on Amazon)

You can access this book by visiting the link below-

http://geni.us/selfconfidence

This will teach you how to build up your self-confidence so you can achieve victories in all areas of your life.

Chapter 8: Overcoming Shyness

If you think that you're struggling with shyness, welcome to the club. I mean even the most outgoing and socially competent person you know is struggling with some level of shyness. It's probably not going to be at the same level as you, it's probably not going to be that extreme but nobody is immune to this.

It's easy to see why this is the case because whenever you're out in public or you're dealing with other people, there is always a chance that you will fall flat on your face. That's right. There's always the risk that you will make a complete and total fool out of yourself.

That risk never goes away regardless of how good you become with people. That's just not going to happen. There is always that possibility, and at the back of your head, you're worried about it. Depending on how you deal with that, it can lead to serious problems or you can continue to do well.

There are two kinds of shyness

When people say that they're shy, they're basically making a blanket statement that doesn't really mean anything. I'm not saying that they don't feel certain things. I'm not saying that they are unclear as to what they're feeling. They're obviously feeling some sort of negative reaction to people. However, there are two kinds of shyness, and if you want to overcome it, you have to be clear as to what type of shyness you are struggling with.

1. Negative Association

The first type of shyness involves some sort of negative association. At some point in the past, you feel that you have made such a fool out of yourself in front of people who you equate or associate being in front of people with that negative feeling.

This negative association remains even though you are a better person now when it comes to social skills. That negative association remains despite the fact that now you are a better speaker.

That association is all in your head. You choose to keep it alive. You choose to continue to link being with people, going out in some sort of open social area with that negative experience.

2. Chemical Imbalance

The other type of shyness is harder to deal with because it's not just in your head. It's not just a simple matter of choice. Instead, there is an actual chemical imbalance in the neurotransmitter of your brain that triggers all sorts of negative physical effects. There are people who are so shy that they get physically sick.

I'm not talking about just feeling uneasy. I'm not talking about wanting to turn around because you are to just so afraid of what would happen. No, we're talking about actual physical symptoms. These people get sick to the point they vomit. They start trembling. In fact, a lot of people drop their knees and assume the fetal position and start rocking.

This is real stuff, and this is due to a chemical imbalance where finding yourself in any kind of open social setting where you're dealing with people triggers a negative chemical response. Your stress hormone levels shoot up, physical symptoms appear and you are trapped in a negative feedback loop.

It starts out with cold sweat. You're basically feeling clammy, and then you're feeling sweat forming and then you start behaving in a less optimal way.

People are not stupid. People can see this. So, they sit up and pay attention, your social performance suffers. They send you signals, and you interpret these in the worst way possible and your physical symptoms get worse and more.

What started out as simple cold sweat becomes buckets of sweat and then you start shaking and, before you know it, you want to throw up. In fact, before you know it, you want to physically turn around and run at full speed in the other direction.

The good news is that chemical imbalances can be fixed. You can't completely get rid of it just by using chemicals, but there are pharmaceutical products currently available that would help you deal with clinical anxiety disorder.

This is an actual clinical diagnosis. You need to see a psychiatrist to get the right medication. You also need to get counseling to lessen the symptoms.

However, you can fix this. This is not a death sentence to your social life. What I'm going to cover in the following sections deal primarily with negative associations because this is what most people suffer from.

Shy people are often victims of one simple Negative Association

It's easy to think that if you are very shy that you are essentially just harboring all these negative associations. You are under the impression that you have so many negative experiences in the past and these all combine together into this really oppressive feeling that you get when you're dealing with strangers, talking to people one-on-one or otherwise just being out there with other people.

What if I told you that is an illusion? What if I told you that there is really just one negative association that it all leads to? Everything else is just really a rehash of that one negative association.

You have to find this. You have to look at the negative experience that you suffered initially. This is what got the ball rolling. This is what triggered the whole sad situation.

The reason you're shy is that you equate being in any kind of social setting or participating in any kind of social activity with a negative experience. There's this unbreakable bond in your mind between the social setting or the social activity with a negative experience.

Now, what's wrong with this picture? You can engage in a social setting today, and there's no guarantee that negative experience will happen. In fact, usually, since you are a bit older, more experienced and more skilled, there's a good chance that the experience will be very positive. However, why do you hang on to this equation of social setting/activity = negative experience?

Break the Iron Link

Please understand that for you to overcome shyness, you have to break this link between a negative experience from the past and social activity now. Basically, what you're doing is you are saying to yourself that since I have a negative experience in the past due to social activity, this means that any social activity now and in the future will predictably result in a negative experience. That's too much of an assumption to make. Most people cannot tell the future.

Furthermore, like I said, you're better equipped now. You're a different person now. So, why beat yourself up unnecessarily by assuming that you will have a negative experience just because you were in some sort of social setting or engaged in a person-to-person social activity?

Break this iron link- Here's how you do it

The people around you did not cause the negative experience. Seriously. Sure, you might be thinking back and focusing on some people laughing, chuckling, pointing fingers, that of thing. However, let me tell you a lot of that stuff is just mental embellishment because the more you remember that negative or painful experience, the more you fill in details. If you're really honest with yourself in many ways, that did not happen, or you just basically blew things out of proportion.

Instead, the negativity can be traced to your reaction to that experience. You interpreted it in the worst way possible, you blew things up out of proportion and you just made things worse.

You need to change your reaction because if you continue to read that experience today, you continue to strengthen that bond or that link between social setting and activity and a negative experience.

Deprogram yourself

How do you deprogram yourself to get out from under this iron rink? I mean this is easy to say but hard to do. I can convince you that this is not a good thing, and you would absolutely, but that agreement is not going to do you much good because the moment a certain mental image flashes in your mind, you can't help but automatically respond in the worst way possible. All the old negative feelings come back over and over again.

Not surprisingly when you find yourself in a social setting, you start behaving the way you normally behave. You feel shy. You feel like you're being judged. You feel that something bad is about to happen. You feel awkward and on and on it goes.

You have to deprogram yourself. The first step to this is to understand that there are different ways to read "negative" social signals. Here's an example from personal experience. I remember going to this fraternity party at a college that my friends and I visit because it's close to my university's campus. We went in and there were really good-looking women there. We're talking about mid-western, corn-fed, blond, blue-eyed all-American women.

One girl looked at my direction and laughed. It was a very hearty laugh, too. I remember sitting there automatically assuming that she was laughing at me. I remember reading her laugh as a judgment of my looks, who I was, where I came from, what I'm about, and the more I focused on her laugh, the more I felt rejected, discouraged, diminished. I felt like an ant.

Well, it turned out, after twenty years, my friends and I had a get-together, that it was not what I remembered it to be. It turned out that when I remember that scene, it got worse and worse because I would fill in the blanks. It's true. She was laughing in my general direction. It's true she was looking at me.

However, one of my friends started dating her, and I didn't know about this because it happened several years after that incident. It turned out she liked me, and she was laughing at the guy behind me who chose to wear his hat in a very obscene way. Well, it worked. He got a lot of attention but, apparently, it was the wrong attention. So, she was laughing.

All this time, I thought this girl was judging me in the worst way possible, and I packed in all sorts of negative readings. Basically, I was saying to myself, "Well, I'm ugly or I'm not attractive enough. Maybe I'm not tall enough. You know, you need to be 6'3". I'm only 6 feet. Maybe I was poor because I wasn't wearing Abercrombie and Fitch" and on and on it goes.

It was a long mental laundry list, and every time I go back to that memory, that list got longer and longer.

However, when I talked to my friend all those years later, that list disappeared, and now I look at that same memory and I feel good about it because she wasn't laughing at me. In fact, she liked me. My friend was telling me that she asked about me. She said, "Who's that tall Polynesian guy you're with? He's sexy."

Do you see the power of mental association? You create a mental prison for yourself just based on your reading of facts and it turns out that we read too much negativity into social signals that we get.

This is why it's really important for you to proactively read memories and current social signals in the best light possible. I'm not saying you should lie to yourself. That's another thing entirely. That doesn't work, but you should look at what actually is going on. Is there a neutral way to read this? Is there something I can do to determine if this is really as negative as I think?

If I had only turned around and seen that my other friend was wearing his hat in a very obnoxiously obscene way, I would have seen the context. I would not have let that memory haunt and negatively impact my self-esteem for so long. Do you see how this works?

You have to do this yourself. This applies to both negative memories that feed into your shyness, and it also applies to what's going on right now. This is not easy, mind you. You are, after all, overwriting a mental habit or a negative association.

The good news is by simply sticking to it, you become more successful and you get closer and closer to permanently change this association.

Another approach would be to do what I did, which was randomly talk to my friend and by chance he let me in on what really happened, and this changed that memory. So, instead of it constantly annoying and degrading my self-confidence, I look back at now as a positive thing or at least it's neutral. Do you see how this works?

So, you have to go through and rummage through your emotional closet, and I'm talking about your past here, and see whether some memories you're hanging onto lead you to this negative association. Remember the facts and see if there's any way you can look at them to at least neutralize them. I'm not saying that you should turn them into a positive thing, but at least find some sort of objective basis for making them more neutral.

Remember: You are always in control

The bottom line here is actually pretty simple. Regardless of whether you're dealing with things from the past or things that are happening in front of you, you are always reading the situation. As the reader, you know you have a lot more control than you give yourself credit for. You read in meaning.

There is such a thing as subjective meaning. Yes, I admit that, but don't ever downplay the importance of subjective reading because things may not be as bad as you remember them. Things may not be as sad as you perceive them to be now.

Avoid the Negative Feedback loop

Given our power to read the worst into our daily activities, please understand that this really becomes almost irresistible because of negative feedback loops. We find ourselves in a situation where we end up reinforcing the very worst readings we can come up with of our daily stimuli. It doesn't have to be that way.

There is such a thing as a positive feedback loop. You can choose to flip the script. You can choose to create an upward spiral instead of a downward one. However, it is a choice.

Unfortunately, exercising that choice, knowing when to do it and how to do it requires effort and you watch repeated failures until you get good at it, but you have to do it. Otherwise, you end up with a negative feedback loop. This is how shyness becomes entrenched.

It becomes stronger and stronger because you feel that it is validated by reality. What you're really doing is you are just engaged in a negative feedback loop. You could have chosen differently. You could have flipped it around.

Here's how it normally works. You focus on your negative reading of the feedback.

For example, you see this really hot member of the opposite sex doing something seemingly directed at you. So, you give it the worst negative reading whatsoever. You interpret it as a complete and total condemnation, dismissal or rejection of who you are as a person. You feel completely unattractive, unwanted, unlovable, etc., etc.

You then feel shy because you don't want to be around other people because you feel that this is the kind of reaction you get. So, you perform badly. This can mean just running away from the social event, or this means going to and just nursing a beer, watching everybody else have a good time. Alternatively, if you at a dance club or an outdoor dance party, you're just dancing around in circles by yourself or with your narrow circle of friends.

This, unfortunately, draws more negative feedback. Well, at least you think they're negative. People will sit up and pay attention. You then interpret it the worst way again, the process repeats itself and you end up digging deeper and deeper into a negative emotional hole.

What do you think happens to your shyness in this context? It gets stronger and stronger. Basically, you're telling yourself, "This is objective proof that social settings are bad and causes me pain, makes me feel unloved, makes me feel unwanted and people can't accept me, there's something wrong with me" and on and on it goes.

There is good news here. You don't have to do it. You don't have to be stuck in that negative feedback loop. In the following chapters, I'm going to teach you how to get out of that emotional hole. See you there.

Chapter 9: Getting Ready To Get Social

Now that you have a clear idea of the negative feedback loop that is keeping your social skills down and holding you back from the kind of social life you would like for yourself, the next step is to get ready. Now, a lot of people might think that this is pretty straightforward. You might think that this is just common sense; no, it isn't.

You have to make sure that you have the right mindset getting into this. Otherwise, you are going to fail again and again. At the very least, you're not going to get the results that you had hoped for. As I mentioned in Chapter 1, you need to get your mind right regarding this whole project. Similarly, you need to get the right mindset so you can succeed in actually taking steps to get social.

Remember: It's not about you

The first thing that you need to understand before you get out there and try out the steps listed below is that it is not about you. I just want to make that clear. Don't take it personally. The problem here is that a lot of people think that when they engage in any kind of social interaction, it's about them getting stuff from other people. It's about them getting out there putting themselves in the spotlight and getting attention.

If this is your position, then it's no surprise that things fall apart sooner rather than later. Oftentimes, things play out in the worst possible. Why? Your ego is front and center. You cannot take this personally because it's not about you. Instead, you have to turn it around. You have to understand that getting social is about them. That's right. It's about other people.

Be genuinely interested in what other people say, what they are about, and what it feels like to be around them. Instead of inwardly focused, where everything is all about you and it's a judgment of your character and values, your priorities should be more outward-focused. Now, this is going to be a little bit difficult. You're going to have such problems because you are so inward-focused. Well, you have to turn them around.

The good news here is that you don't have to be outward-focused all the time. This doesn't have to take place all day every day. Just be outward-focused enough at least for a limited period of time. It doesn't have to be long, but the great thing here is that you can start with a fairly short period of time and then scale it up over time.

The Secret? Be curious about others

So what is the secret to turning your focus from an internal one to something more others-directed? Well, it actually boils down to simple curiosity. Choose to be curious about others. Be truly interested in learning about them. Try to get excited about actually being with different people.

Instead of constantly trying to draw attention to yourself or focusing on what's important to you, step outside your ego for quite some time and simply enjoy being with them. Allow yourself to be drawn to their differences. It doesn't have to be scary. It doesn't have to be rare. It doesn't have to be intimidating.

Why do you need to do this?

Well, people are smarter than you think. People can tell if you are truly interested, and this helps ease social interaction both for them and you. When people feel that you truly care about what they have to say, they open up more. They become accepting of you. This, in turn, helps you mellow out, and the social interaction becomes smoother and smoother.

The reason why you are struggling with the social situation is usually the opposite. People have their defenses up, and you don't really give them any reasons to lower their guard, so you create a downward spiral. You already know this. This negative feedback loop is very real and it hurts your ability to improve your social skills. See chapter 8's discussion on this.

Set yourself at ease by being prepared

So how exactly do you allow yourself to be more outward-focused and to be more comfortable around other people? There are simple tricks you can use. Now, what I will teach you below doesn't apply across the board. In many cases, some tips won't apply, but do the best you can.

First, if you can, go to the place where the social event will take place. For example, if you are going to be giving a speech in front of a lot of people, it helps tremendously to go to that place first and feel your way around. There's absolutely nobody there, but in your mind, you gain some level of familiarity. This is not a totally alien territory to you.

Gain familiarity with the place and the layout. Try to position your body as you move in front of the crowd that will appear. This goes a long way in losing that quote "fish out of the water." feeling. Try to look at the place from many different angles. Try to imagine the crowd there and come up with some coping mechanisms that would make it feel more familiar.

Pump yourself up by remembering the last successful social event you are in

Right before the event, you probably would have many butterflies in your stomach. This is perfectly natural. Do yourself a big favor and pump yourself up by thinking back to the last successful social event you were in. Maybe you met somebody new. Maybe you got people to laugh at your jokes. Maybe you hit it off pretty well to some people.

It doesn't have to be big. It doesn't have to be hugely successful. As long as it is some sort of success, that's good enough. Keep that in your mind. Allow yourself to be emotionally pumped up by that experience. Highlight and focus on the emotional state you had then. It felt good, right? Allow yourself to feel good. Emphasize it. Highlight it. Exaggerate it and translate it to your feelings now.

If you do this right, you can't help but feel hopeful, encourage, and inspired today. This is a great thing because it beats the hell out of feeling stuck or feeling like you don't know what you're doing. If you keep this up, eventually you will instantly snap into the mindset that you need to have. What mindset is this? Well, you just need to focus on the phrase, "I've done this before and I can do it again." That's the mindset you need to be in because once you're there, things start to flow.

Always remember your core competence

As you prepare for the social engagement, remember your core competence. This is the basis of your self-worth. You know you are worthy because you're competent in certain things. You're not a complete and total loser. Once you have a clear idea of your self-worth and you have played it up in your mind, your self-confidence starts to flow. You say to yourself, "Well, I am competent in certain things and due to this confidence, I'm worth something. If I'm worth something, then I'm not all that bad. I can be capable. I can do certain things right. I'm not so bad. I'm not doomed to fail."

When you do this, avoid the common trap of setting impossible standards for yourself. When forming this involves the scale. You don't have to make millions of dollars to consider yourself successful. You don't have to go home with a supermodel each and every night to consider yourself decent-looking or good looking. Do you see how this works? Avoid setting impossible standards because that's how you undermine and sabotage yourself.

Practice breathing exercises

Breathe deeply and slowly. Slow things down. Allow that sense of relaxation to enter your mind and then let it sink to your emotions. Keep repeating that slow breathing pattern until you have calmed down. Once you are relaxed, go through the mental exercises I describe above and repeat the process. At the end of this process, you should be both relaxed and confident at the same time.

Use the "V for victory Posture"

According to scientific research, when people raise their arms up in the air like a boxer winning a prized match, this releases chemical signals that boost confidence and energy. Interestingly enough, it also sends social signals to other people around and they reflect that energy to you. This is not a solo thing.

Find a way to do this V Posture as you tour the place where the social event will be or once you are already at the place. When you do this, you boost your confidence, your energy levels go up, and you also draw the positive social response. It is no surprise that people react that way because this is an alpha pose.

Cap it off by doing this

By this point. you should be feeling very good. You should be feeling pumped up and you are ready to get into the zone. This is where things start to flow. This is where the magic happens. However, before you jump in, realize that the worst case scenario is nothing. I need you to focus on this. What's the worst thing that can happen? People laugh; so what? They laugh at so many other things as well. People shun you and turn their backs; been there done that. The deal doesn't get approved; so what? You don't have a deal right now. You're just back to where you came from, back to where you are. Where's the big loss?

I need you to go through every fear you may have regarding the worst-case scenario and just demolish them because ultimately, there's nothing to fear. How bad can things get? Oftentimes, we blow up the worst- case scenario in our mind and make things harder on ourselves. In reality, we're just scared of our shadows. We're just scared of the things that could happen, but ultimately, even if they come to pass, not match changes.

If you think women will think you are looser, well, how is that any different from what's going on now? If you think you will be rejected because a female thinks you are ugly, how's that any different from what you have now? You have to remember that to some people, you will be really good-looking. To others, you'll be average, and to some, you'll be ugly. That's the way life is.

I mean Leonardo dicaprio, as famous of a Hollywood star as he is, is flat-out repugnant to some women. That's how statistical distributions work. So get over it. The whole worst case scenario is a whole lot of nothing. Keep focusing on that. It's not enough to be relaxed. It's not enough to be pumped up and confident, you also have also to look at the worst-case scenario because once that happens, your fear will no longer have a hold on you. You are free to get into the zone.

Chapter 10: Getting Into The Zone

Now that you are in a social setting, it's time to shine. This is where the tire meets the road. The good news is that it is easier than you think. Here is a step-by-step approach to get into the zone, stay in there and maximize your wins. Look for easy wins. The first thing that you need to do is to look for the easy stuff. This is a low-hanging fruit as far as social validation and positive feedback loops are concerned.

First, smile to the crowd. That's all you need to do - Flash a smile. Now, the smile must come from the heart. It has to be genuine. You can't force it. You can't look like a hostage that is forced to grin because there's a gun at the back of his head. That's not going to work. The smile has to be authentic.

Smile to the person in front of you or at the crowd that you are about to give a speech to. When you do that, someone somehow, someway, at some time will smile back. Why? This is human nature. This is called reciprocity. We have this reflex burned into our DNA. When somebody does something to us, at some point or another we reflect that action on them.

Have you ever noticed that when somebody is kind to you, you feel the urge to be kind back to them? That's how normal people respond. Well, you can override it by being extremely shy or being extremely self-conscious, but there is that drive. That's not going to go away anytime soon.

Accordingly, when someone smiles back, don't be surprised. This is reciprocity in action. When you get that signal, count it as a win and use the positive energy that you get when somebody reflects your smile to smile even more. Guess what will happen? Somebody else from the crowd will smile back at you. Keep repeating this. What you're doing is you're "harvesting" good vibes from the crowd. They help pump you up. They help create this upward spiral of confidence in you.

Remember to smile authentically

I can't emphasize this enough. I know I've said it already, but I need to say it again. Smile from the heart. How do you know if your smile is real? Well, it's actually simple - people can tell by your eyes. According to research studies, when people are really smiling, their eyes squint. The corners of their eyes go up that it looks like they're squinting. That's how you know the person is not faking it.

You have to remember that people are watching you. They are mindful. They're not going to be obvious about it, but people are paying attention to you. There is such a thing as crowd intelligence. So smile from the heart. Don't fake it. The good news is once people bounce your smile back to you, it becomes more and more authentic and it becomes easier and easier for you to truly smile from the heart.

Next, make it a point to greet people and mention their names. Yes, even if you are giving a speech in front of a crowd point to people you know and say, "Hey, how are you doing?" or "Hi Bob! how are you?.", "Hey James, thanks for showing up. Thanks for coming."

It sets people at ease, and guess what? You're not just creating a rapport with the people you're singling out and pointing to and smiling with. The crowd also pays attention. They make judgments. They say, "Okay, this guy is comfortable. This guy knows people and acknowledges people. Let me give this person the benefit of the doubt."

This creates a sense of ease not just with people you're conversing with, but with the crowd in general. Guess what happens? That's right. It's like the "smile effect". When you set people at ease, their sense of ease bounces back at you and you feel more at ease. You then bounce this back and this creates mutual comfort.

You see how does it work? It's not that complicated. In fact, you're probably doing it at some level or other. What's different is that you are going to have to choose to be more conscious about this process.

Look at people in the eye with smiling eyes

When you are in a one-to-one or one-to-few type of social interaction, look at people in the eye. Now, I'm not saying you should freak them out like jutting your jaw forward and leaning forward to invade their space. I'm not saying that you should talk to them like Marlon Brando talked to the camera in Apocalypse Now. That's going to send all the wrong signals. Don't do that.

Instead, look at people in the eye with smiling eyes. Basically, your eyes are saying, "You are safe with me." or, "I'm a friend." This creates mutual comfort. Of course, you have to pair this with a smile and you have to smile from the heart. But when you send all these signals, people are comforted. They feel at ease. You're not the enemy. You're not somebody they should have their defenses up about. They don't have to have their guard up. They can interact with you on an open level.

Project confidence

Now that you are at ease with people around you, the next step is to project confidence. This is crucial because if you want people to like you, admire you, or respect you, you have to project a sense that you know what you are doing, you know what you're capable of, and you are worth hanging out with.

Now, this is hard to do with the words coming out of your mouth because if you did that, people would say, "This person is full of himself. He likes to boast. I bet this due to this fake." Don't do that because you might provoke all sorts of negative responses and negative reactions. Whatever comfort you've managed to build up prior to this point will just go down the toilet.

Instead, project confidence with your body language. How do you do this? well, put your hands on your hips. Open your arms and lean in slightly with your shoulders as you listen to people attentively. Turn your head slightly as you look them in the eye when they talk to you.

This means you are taking them seriously. This means that you are trying to tune in closely to what they say. They feel that they matter when you do this. They perceive your real interest so they are more drawn to you.

Not only should you use body language to send signals out, you should also draw physical signal from others. When people have their hands on their hips, or they are talking to you intently and their body language shows this, don't interpret this is a threat. This is not a competition. Instead, allow it to pump you up even more so you are more physically demonstrative about the attention you are giving them.

The secret? Do not be afraid to make the first move

Now, all of the above is awesome. But you cannot just lean back and wait for somebody to show up and then you go through the steps I've described above. You have to take the initiative. You have to go out there and make the first move.

Now, a lot of people who have all sorts of misconceptions and misunderstanding about this. They think they have to have some sort of amazing opening line. In the context of meeting somebody new, a lot of guys are under the impression that they should have a clever pickup line. That's bunked. okay? There's no need for that.

Just simply say, "Hello! My name is (Fill in the blanks.)." This is good enough because it's not the opening line that gets the ball rolling. It's not the pickup line that makes you attractive or worth talking to. Instead, it's the climate of comfort you produce.

Understand this. Don't think that there is some sort of magical line you just need to recite and all of a sudden, business deals are closed or chicks come out-out of nowhere wanting to go home with you. It doesn't work that way. That's magical thinking.

Instead, social rapport is a complete experience. There are many different parts working together. They're many pieces of the puzzle that need to be aligned properly. Think of it as a nice dance. You have to move with your partner in a certain way. You have to pay attention to what they do so you can move accordingly, and on and on it goes. It's a two-way street. It's not just you wanting something and jumping in with both feet to get it. It doesn't work that way.

Chapter 11: Speak Confidently

In the previous chapter, we talked about the things that you do with your body. We talked about body language and eye contact among other things. In this chapter, I'm going to focus on the things you're going to be doing with your mouth. You have to understand that speech is a crucial part of any social interaction. You have to learn how to be a good conversationalist. You have to learn the art of small talk.

Please understand that according to behavioral psychologists, human beings "groom" each other through conversations. Have you ever watched any wildlife channel and seen chimpanzees picking bugs off each other's fur? That's how they groom each other. That's not a random activity. The more they do that, the stronger their group's social ties become. That's how everybody gets along.

Humans do the same thing, but instead of picking lies off each other's hair, we talk to each other. That's how we groom each other. That's how we set each other at ease and how we strengthen our social bonds. In any type of social situation, regardless of whether you already know people or you just met them, you need to groom them as well. Thankfully, it's not that hard as you think.

The secret to good conversations

Now that you know how central talking to others is, how do you become a good conversationalist? How do you create a situation where people walk away saying to themselves, "That person is awesome to talk to."? Well, it's actually easier than you think. Here's the secret that I use that works like a charm.

Get others to talk about themselves. Let me tell you, people love to talk about themselves. There is one subject in the world that they never get tired of, and that is themselves. They talk about what's going on in their lives. They talk about their hobbies. They talk about their projects. They talk about their successes. Some people like to talk about their failures, challenges, and struggles. That's okay too.

Whatever the case may be, it all leads back to the same place. They talk about themselves. It's all about "I", "me", "mine", and guess what? That is awesome because the more they talk about themselves, the less time you have to actually talk. You can just talk with them in a way that they keep talking about the things that are important to them. All you feedback is aimed at one thing and one thing only: get them to talk more.

How do you do this? Pay attention to what they say and ask follow-up questions. Try to get them to connect the dots with the things that they say. Also, feel free to repeat what they say and summarize certain things. The key here is to get them to keep talking, talking, and talking.

Now, this doesn't mean that you're just going to sit back and let all this info get into one ear and out to the other. That's not going to work. You have to actually listen because when they talk, they give away valuable clues as to who they are, what's important to them, what their hopes and dreams are; you know, the stuff that makes people human. Pay attention. It's also important to note that the more they talk, the more comfortable they feel around you.

Let people know that you are listening

It's one thing to get people to talk; it's another to get them to feel good about you while they are talking. While they can feel comfortable, you want them to feel good. The way to do this, of course, is to let them know that you are listening. Here are some tips on how to make that happen.

First, you need to recap and summarize. Somebody may be telling a long, convoluted and complicated story regarding their grandmother being related to some sort of noble in Eastern Europe and how this has impacted their desire to form a venture or startup company like Silicon Valley, which then leads to their initial failures and their frustrations, etcetera, etcetera.

It's long and convoluted, but interesting. So what you do is you recap the stuff that you think is most important to them and also summarize the story in a way that reflects your interests. Focus on what you're excited about and recap with short, compact summary that includes stuff that is important to them.

People appreciate this because they are put on notice that this person is actually listening to me. This person finds me interesting enough to invest brain cells in summarizing what I just said. You've instantly become more interesting to them.

Another approach you can try is to tie in what they are saying now with what they have said before. For example, if somebody is saying that they are currently working at Goldman Sachs as an investment banker, you may want to tie this into the internship that they have mentioned earlier at another investment broker house, as well as some graduate classes that they took.

When you do this, you are reminding the person that he or she is not just spouting off information. You are telling them in very clear terms that what they say is important enough to keep track of. Also, you demonstrate to them that they are important enough to you for you to try to figure them out. Most people would love the attention.

Now, those people who have something to hide, and I'm talking about people who are lying, will get freaked out by this. If you are a liar, you basically have to continue lying to cover up inconsistencies, and it's really hard to keep up an elaborate story. Eventually, that will catch up to you. It will all fall apart with one false move, kind of like a house of cards.

For normal people, however, this is a good thing because you're actually telling them that what they are saying is important to you because they are important to you. They matter to you. They can't help but feel appreciation.

Also, you should ask a lot of questions. These questions must not be interrogatory in nature. You should not make them feel that they are deposed by an opposing counsel in a lawsuit. Don't make them feel that they are in court and being cross-examined. That's the wrong impression. Just ask gentle questions that try to draw them. Also, ask open-ended questions that can lead to other areas of discussion.

Finally, make it clear that they are taking the stage. You're not there to judge them. You're not there to hog the spotlight. For example, if somebody is talking about the new Porsche that they've bought,
don't just cut in and say, "Well, I just bought a new Ferrari. What a coincidence." How do you think that will make the person feel? He or she is proud of his or her new possession. Let them take the center stage. They are entitled to their pride.

If you are to constantly butt in and say, "Well, here's what I did..." or "Here's what I got...", you are essentially trying to cancel their right to feel good about whatever it is they have achieved. I see this a lot in terms of personal achievement. When somebody would say, "After graduating from New York University, I went on to graduate school." Then, somebody cuts in and says, "Well, I went to Harvard." or "I went to Berkeley."

Do you see the disconnect? Instead of drawing the person out making them feel more comfortable as they relay their story and claim their place on the stage, you basically shut them down. You basically try to create some sort of perspective wherein their achievement, as awesome as it is, does not look as good as before. How do you think people would respond? Would you react positively if that was done to you? My point exactly. Don't do that.

Avoid the temptation to step into the conversation

Let's face it. We come across people who say a lot of stupid things. That's part of life because guess what? You do it too. Everybody is not immune to this. At some point at some time, we say stupid stuff. We say the wrong things at the wrong time and they produce the wrong impressions. That's how people are. This is part of the human condition. Nobody is perfect.

Unfortunately, you make things worse when you step into the conversation because your actions, even though you did not intend to, point these problem areas out. By simply talking about yourself and your accomplishments, you suck out the Oxygen from the conversation.

The key here is to get them to talk about what excites them. This is your way of letting them introduce themselves to you so they can tell you in so many words what their values are, their priorities, what they are about their hopes and dreams and what they have done.

This is important stuff if you really want to get to know somebody. But if you keep talking about yourself, you are pushing them away. You are robbing the conversation of its Oxygen. Instead of allowing the conversation to enable you to learn about other people, it goes back to your default position, which is that it's all about you.

Avoid the tendency to step on the conversation in any way. Be responsive. When somebody says something interesting, just say, "Oh! That is interesting! Wow!" The key here is to be fully expressive. So when you say, "Uh-huh?!" and you're nodding your head or you have this look in your eye that you're seriously paying attention, that draws them in. That stimulates them to share even more.

So don't hold back about nodding your head. Please understand that just because you're nodding your head, it doesn't mean that you agree with what they're saying. When somebody may be saying something really horrible, you nod your head but you also have to send him other signals. This means that you're not agreeing with what they are saying. It's not saying that you want to do what they did. o

Instead, it just shows that you are at the moment. Also, don't hold back from asking very detailed questions. The more detailed the questions, the better. Why? This shows in certain terms that you are taking them seriously and are really into what they are saying.

Now, with that said, you can't take the conversation so seriously that everything becomes heavy. This is where jokes come in. At some point when people talk, there are certain parts where they make light points. You're not exactly launching into a formal joke, but it's a light area. Learn how to spot the difference between heavy conversation and light points.

Also, spot the difference between jokes and light points. There are certain people who have personalities that are more comfortable with telling jokes. Be aware of this. Many people like to crack jokes. So what do you do? You laugh at their jokes. Just don't overdo it. Because if you overdo it, it's obvious that you're just faking it. Basically, you're insulting the person. In fact, it may come out like mockery. Learn how to spot their jokes and respond appropriately.

Also, other people make light points not so much because they want to make a joke. Oftentimes, they do this to highlight their wit and intelligence. Stop this and respond appropriately. Now, here's the thing. Some jokes are really funny. In that respect, laugh heartily. if the joke is not funny, just nod your head and say, "Hmm, okay." Basically, you're telling them you get it. You're trying to tell a joke, but it's not that funny. But you're not going to insult them.

Do you see how this works? There is a nuance somewhere, so you have to catch the nuance. Don't overdo any of these because any kind of overreaction will expose you as a fake.

The secret to effective conversations about yourself

Now, in certain parts of the conversation, the topic will turn to you. When that happens, always talk about the things that you know. The rest, you're just going to reserve questions. When making a claim or an assertion, stick to it now. Try to get away from making all sorts of wild claim, speculation or theory because the more you do that, the more you come off as a crackpot. The more you will make an impression that you're not really a disciplined thinker.

I'm not saying that it's totally and completely wrong. In certain contexts, usually when talking about art, creativity, or you're talking about weird theories, feel free to knock yourself out with your speculative side. But in a course of a normal conversation, try to stick with what you actually know.

Now, even if you do that, there are still going to be situations where people will correct you because maybe you've overlooked the fact. Maybe you focused too much on one end of an argument that you didn't know that there are other facts at play. So when people do this, don't take it as an insult. Instead, look at it for what it is. It is a teachable moment. It's there to help you. It's there to increase your level of knowledge.

Get ready to be corrected. There's nothing wrong with it. It doesn't mean you're dumb or less of a person. People get corrected all the time. It's called education. when people do this and they have a point, acknowledge it. Don't brush it off. Don't say to yourself, "You're an idiot. You're wrong." No!

If they've made a good argument and it's backed by facts, accept it. Again, it doesn't mean that you lost and they won. It just means you learned something new. Isn't that awesome?

Get ready to accept what others say and tie it in with what you know. For example, if you're arguing about something and somebody said, "Well, this fact pretty much disproves what you are saying." Instead of beating each other up regarding that fact, as long as you know that that fact is correct, accept it and tie it in with what you are saying.

The safer approach here, of course, is to focus less on making a claim. Usually, when people make claims, they're really trying to "prove their intelligence". Understand that this conversation is not about winning. Instead, it's making people more comfortable around you making them want to like you more.

Know your priorities. Know the point of the conversation. It's about building bridges, not showcasing how much better you are than them. Accordingly, step away from making claims or proving intelligence. Instead, ask a lot of questions. Get answers, try to repack them, then ask more questions.

When you do this, you turn the conversation around. It's no longer about you, how intelligent you are, how many toys you own, how much more money you make, etcetera, etcetera. Instead, it's all about them. It highlights your interest in them - what's going on in their lives, what's important to them, what they have, how you can help them, so on and so forth. When you do this, people feel comfortable. Bonds are created. Rapport is generated.

Chapter 12: Occupy The Same Emotional Space

In the previous 2 chapters, we talked about body language and speech patterns in great conversations. In this chapter, we are going to talk about emotional conversations.

Believe it or not, the vast majority of signals you send to somebody in the course of the conversation does not involve the words you say. I know, that sounds crazy because usually, people think about the words leaving their mouths. Well, that's actually the most conscious part of communication. There's a lot of value in that, but you need to go beyond the obvious.

You're actually saying a lot of non-verbal signals. By being mindful of non-verbal signals, you become a better communicator. Here's what you need to do.

Look people in the eye

I don't know about you, but the last time I talked to somebody who didn't look me in the eye, I felt insulted. I felt that this person was trying to hide something. This person showed disrespect because if you truly consider the person in front of you worthy of talking, you would look them in the eye. Of course, you have to do this with smiling eyes.

You can't look at them the same way Manny Pacquaio looked at Floyd Mayweather during their prized fight face-off. You know, you lift your chin up and look at them down your nose. That is not the kind of eye contact I'm talking about.

Look people in the eye with smiling eyes. This shows them in no uncertain terms that they are important, they matter, and this conversation is important to you. You are not blowing them off. This is not an afterthought. This is not a conversation that you're forced to have. This is real to you. It's that important.

Emote with your eyes

I see this a lot with my wife. When she talks to people, she's not just saying things with her words. You can easily tell what she means when you like in her eyes because she has this amazing emotional vocabulary. It's not just with the positioning of her eyes, but the muscle around her eyes. You can tell exactly whether she's upset, frustrated, happy, expectant, hopeful, inspired, and it's all in her eyes.

You can do it too. The thing here is to be conscious of all the signals you are sending with your face because facial expression goes a long way. You can say the kindest, most uplifting and most gratifying words in history, but if your face looks like you're in the middle of a funeral, it's really not going to go over well.

Emote with your tone of voice

How you say something is just as important as what you have to say. When you emote with your tone of voice, you say so many things. You position the text of your speech. You set context and expectations. You also set limits. Your tone of voice is very important. Be mindful of it.

I know you're reading this, so it seems like I'm speaking in one tone, but you need to get past that. You need to imagine yourself speaking to a person and be aware of the contrasts between the words in printed form and the words as received by a person's ears. These are two totally different things.

This also highlights why you should be very careful in how to send emails. Emails do not have tones. You may have all the love, compassion and care in your heart when you type something out, but all bets are off when it reaches the other end because there is no tone. This is why emojis were invented.

Emote with the tone of your voice. Use it as a tool and be mindful of it. You must use it to emphasize and give shape to whatever it is you're saying.

Remember: This is not a competition nor it is combat

When you're in the same emotional space, it's very easy to feel touchy. It's very easy to feel like you're on the spot and you have to defend yourself. Welcome to the club! This is human nature, but you need to override this.

Understand that when you're engaged in a conversation, you're trying to make people comfortable around you. Now, there are certain discussions where it makes perfect sense for you to be combative. But if you're trying to meet somebody new or you're trying to get a deal going, you need to make people comfortable.

How do you make this happen? Well, you can do this by first allowing yourself to be comfortable. Again, we're talking about the emotional space. You have to remember that people read you emotionally. They're not just reading you textually based on the words you say. They don't just pay attention to these signals you're sending through your body language. They are also reading you emotionally.

You can consider this the Sixth sense. Some people are better at it than others. Psychologists call it emotional intelligence. Regardless of how you label it or how aware you are of it, you need to understand that this is a thing. This is real. And oftentimes, the best way to make people comfortable around you emotionally is to be comfortable yourself.

The more comfortable they are, the more comfortable they feel. The more comfortable they get, the more comfortable you feel. This goes on and on. You reinforce each other's comfort level.

Now, please understand that this works in the opposite direction as well. If you're uncomfortable, sooner or later, people around you will feel uncomfortable. Once you detect that they're not really having that good of a time, you feel even more upset, discouraged, diminished, stressed out, or anxious. You then send out signals, and this leads to a downward spiral. Down and down it goes.

The good news is that it's your choice. When you get in there, you set the tone. Be comfortable. How do you do this? Well, always remember what you're not trying to achieve. You're not trying to be right. You're not trying to win a debate. You're not trying to interrogate. Understand this. These do not have any place in your mission.

Again, in certain conversations, this makes a lot of sense. For example, if you're supervising and you caught somebody stealing, you're going to have to engage in these types of conversations but not now. You're trying to meet a member of the opposite sex. You're on your second date and you're trying to know each other more. You may be in a job interview or in a business networking meeting. The name of the game is a comfort.

It's okay to overreact at certain times

Believe it or not, there are certain times in a conversation where it makes a lot of sense to overreact. By overreacting, I'm talking about exaggerated emotional responses. Again, don't go overboard because there is a line that you can cross where your overreaction comes off as mockery. You're basically making the person feel stupid. You're rejecting the person. You're making them feel that somehow or someway, they are inferior. That's not the kind of impression you should be trying to create.

You're trying to get people feel that they matter, they are accepted, and they can get comfortable with you. So understand this background when choosing to overreact. It's okay to do that, but there are limits.

So when is it okay to overreact? Well, when people are telling a story, it's probably a good time. When you overreact, you're basically telling them, "Whoah! I'm with you." or "Wow! That's really amazing." You're basically complimenting them. You must do this sincerely and authentically. You're not just faking it until you make it.

Also, when people are trying to get you in on a joke. Now, this is not kind of like a public joke, where it's obvious that they're joking. Instead, they have an internal joke, and they're trying to figure out in their mind whether you can get it or not. In other words, are you one of them?

This is one of the most powerful ways to build rapport because a lot of powerful people operate at this level. They say, "Is this guy or this woman one of us?" Let's test this person. Can they get the inside joke?

Sometimes, the joke takes the form of a look, with a smile on their face. When you bounce it back to them, they would instantly know that you're on the same mental wavelength. All of a sudden, you're a friend. You're no longer this stranger.

Regardless if you are overreacting to a story or a joke, understand that you should not overdo it. I cannot repeat this enough because if you overdo it, you come off like you're mocking the person. I remember one time when somebody cracked a joke. It was a pretty mild joke, but I blew up laughing.

Instead of the person appreciating that I was laughing, he took it as an insult. Basically, he thought that I was making fun of him for making such an ill-timed joke.

So, instead of building a wall and mutual comfort, it built a great wall before us. The person was thinking, "This person is always judging me. This person is thinking he is so superior to me. Forget this person."

Do you see where I am coming from here? I did not have any malice. I actually really liked the joke but I forgot that threshold. Don't go over that threshold. You don't want to come off as mocking. Instead of a being a friend, the relationship gets frozen and you just remain strangers to each other.

The power of inside references

After you have been talking to someone for a while, remember what they said early on and try to refer to it. This is a very powerful conversational tool because this puts them on notice that you understand them. This puts them on notice that you are truly paying attention and that you have taken this to a personal level. This is not just something that you listen to with one ear and out it goes out the other ear.

They feel that "Wow! This person really gets me." Now, here is the trick. You can't do this with a trivial issue. For example, I remember going out on a date with this very amazing woman. I mean she was a Washington lawyer, really well-paid, really good-looking, I'm talking about model quality. She lived in the East Coast.

Things were going well as we were walking up a hill in San Francisco. Then, she was telling me that when she was a kid, the most comforting memories she had was that she actually lived in a room in her parents' home, where there were a washer and dryer. At first, she wasn't really all that happy because a washer and dryer obviously can be quite noisy. But eventually, she would always look forward to that comforting, rocking motion with the dryer and it's color blue.

As the conversation went on, I then referred back to the color of the dryer. Basically, I put her on notice that with all these things that you're talking about, you just focused on the color of the dryer instead of the fact that you had this really personal piece of info that you shared with me about being comforted by the rocking motion of the dryer.

It doesn't really matter what color it is. So it kind of cheapened things. It kind of dialed back the intimacy that we were building and the conversation was not as good from that point on.

So please understand that inside references are a double-edged sword. They can work for you really well, but if you botch them up, you can freeze the conversation. You can't focus on a trivial issue when you do this. If you pull this off properly, inside references make you more likable. You'll basically reach a point where a person would say, "You know something about me that other people don't because you made the effort. I like you because of that." So do you see how this works?

Chapter 13: Tap the Power of Similarity

Imagine you and your friends walking through a savannah in Africa thousands of years ago. Now, imagine yourselves looking up into the distance and you see a group of people that look very different from you. They wore completely different clothing, they have different head masks, and they look like they're carrying weapons. Well, you're also carrying weapons. You also have your own protective gear on.

This is alarming because they don't look like their part of your trap. They don't look like part of their groups in regions you are most familiar with. What do you think the outcome would be? Now, this has a strong survival mechanism because if you come across people who are similar to you and you help each other, chances are your collective genes will make it to the next generations.

What I want you to get in the story is the fact that when people are similar to each other, there is a long tradition of mutual assistance, support, and resource sharing. This, of course, leads to greater survival. This is hard to shake off. This is pretty much burned in our DNA. We can't escape it.

There's a strong urge to help and be more open to people who look like us, talk like us, and act like us. That's thousands of years' worth of conditioning. It's very hard to overcome. You need to tap into this phenomenon so you can become more effectively social. This is called the power of similarity. People tend to like those who are similar to them.

What do we focus on? Well, we focus on looks, language, the way of speaking, values, and priorities. Again, this is evolutionary in origin. This is something that you can easily override. You can overcome it but it takes discipline and training. That's how we are oriented. We tend to support people who look more like us.

Tap the power of similarity

So how do you tap into this power of similarity? One of the easiest ways to do it is to simply mirror who you're talking to. You don't have to be of the same race. You don't have to come from the same country of origin nor do you have to have the same religion. You don't have to have any of those.

Instead, you just mirror who they are in front of you. How? Well, mirror what they talk about. For example, if they are talking about travel stories, tell travel stories. If the person is talking about cars, then talk about cars. They will appreciate this. At the back of their minds, they are thinking, "This person has similar interests as me. This person is not all that different. I'm beginning to like this person because he is similar to me."

Also, you should consider mirroring how they talk. When somebody is talking about cars, for example, you are probably talking at a certain pace. They are using certain words. They are painting certain scenarios. Mirror this.

Now here is the secret, do not be obvious. You should do it but don't give yourself away. Again, just like with blowing a joke, by overreacting, you come off as mocking. When you're obviously mirroring how another person talks, similarly you should mirror their body language. When people lean forward and have their arms crossed, when they look at you and are leaning at you like they're sharing a secret, copy that a little bit, but don't overdo it.

Again, you don't want any of this to blow up in your face. You don't want to come off as somebody who is just mocking who you are talking to. Do the same emotional language. When you do this, you trigger the power of similarity. At the back of their heads, they think to themselves, "Well, this person talks about the same stuff that I talk about. This person is similar to how I talk. This person's body language is somewhat similar to mine. They are emotionally engaged the same way I am.

This person may not be all that different. This person is likable. Now, again, this really all boils down to how far you are going to take this. You don't want to be a cartoon. You don't want to caricaturize the other person. That's going to have the opposite effect. Tapping the power of similarity is crucial. This gives you a competitive advantage over everybody else who's trying to connect with that person.

Most people are lazy. Seriously, they also don't have that much time. So what do they do? They play a game where they say, "Either you get it or you don't. If you don't get it, too bad. Maybe next time." Well, you don't have that luxury. By stimulating the power of similarity, you're making efforts to connect with this person on a deep, psychological level. You're proactively taking steps towards their direction. You're not taking this "Take it or leave it" game. They don't have to come to you; you come to them.

Chapter 14: Don't Underestimate The Power of Stories

If you want to truly deepen your interaction with other people, don't forget to tell stories. You might think that you are a lousy story teller. You might even think that you don't really have any interesting stories to tell. Well, think again. Most people do have stories to tell. They just don't know it. They have facts, memories, images in their head about past experiences. These are the raw ingredients of stories. You need to tell stories if you want people to find you interesting.

You have to understand that the human mind organizes the world and all the information it contains through stories. That's how we make sense of our world, otherwise, we're just going to go crazy because we have all this stimuli that we are exposed to every single day and there is no way for us to logically make sense of them.

Human beings have to process the world in the form of stories and this is why you need to communicate using the same format. People love to hear stories. It organizes reality. It's easier to process. It also enables people to peek into or get an understanding of what's important to you. They get an inside look of how your personality works. Best of all, stories provide some sort of escape.

When somebody's telling a story, they're obviously not describing things are happening right in front of them. Instead, they direct your attention to something that happened sometime in the past or they tell a story about what could possibly happen in the future. Either way you look at it, you are transported somewhere different from the here and now.

You can't help but be entertained because that is the definition of entertainment. It takes you away from what you are perceiving now. Your mind, your psychological processes, your logical reasoning faculties, and your emotions are transported. Tell stories.

You don't have to be a master story-teller. You don't have to be the next Mark Twain. The moment you tell a story, most people will find some hooks in the material that you are sharing to hang on to. That's how powerful stories are.

Let them go first

As important as it is to tell stories, it's also important to understand proper etiquette. There is etiquette governing stories, believe it or not. The rule that I follow and which has served me quite well for all these years is to let the other person go first. Encourage them to tell a story.

This is a very good strategic move because you end up following their lead. You end up using their story as a pattern. Why is this important? When somebody tells a story, they're making many different choices. They are focusing on one topic over others. They are also focusing on telling that story a certain way instead of alternative narration. Pay attention to this because this is the pattern that you will follow. This is part of the mirroring process like people who are similar to them.

If you tell stories that are somewhat similar to how they tell stories, you can't help but be more likable in their eyes. Follow their lead. At the very least, the stories that they tell you let you know what kind of stories they like. It also lets you know how they craft together a narrative. It tells you about their priorities, values and, of course, their experiences. They're saying all these things. You just have to open your ears and pay attention to what they're telling you. In fact, you may be picking up on certain clues that they themselves aren't aware of.

You also get to know what kind of details they focus on. This is very important. The details somebody spends a lot of time on highlights their values. You get to understand what their priorities are. Most importantly, you now have enough information to put together your own story for their consumption.

Tell your story right

Why are you going through all these? Why are you trying to mirror the other person's narration style? Why are you paying attention to what they're saying and picking it apart to inspire you to say the right things at the right time?

Well, it all boils down to making others comfortable. Basically, you are getting all these clues and packing them into your story when it's your turn to speak. You are enabling yourself to be more comfortable. How? You know that this is what they like. It gives you comfort to know that you know what they like. This, in turn, enables them to be comfortable around you. The more comfortable they are, the more comfortable you get, the stories flow and everybody gets even more and more comfortable. It's all about following their lead.

When it's time for you to tell a story, lay out the story in your mind first. What are the most important points? What came first? What happens in the middle? What does it mean? How does it lay out? What happens at the end? Now that you have a fairly clear idea of the story, look for the inflection points. These are the twists and turns of the plot. These are invitations for the listener to get emotionally engaged.

When you tell your story, exaggerate your emotions to help the narration. If you're expressing shock because there's something unexpected that happened in the story, look shocked. Open your eyes and your mouth. If there's something scary or there's something disgusting, angering or funny, clue the listener in through the emotional cues you are sending him or her.

Also, punctuate your stories with certain questions. These can be rhetorical questions or they can be actual questions. Whatever questions you use, employ them to draw people in. Basically, when you ask a question while you're telling a story, you're getting people to buy in. You're basically telling them, "Are you paying attention? You get this?" When they answer, you go through your story.

If you do everything well, they not only intellectually buy in, but they are also emotionally engaged in the story. Make sure that you always bounce the story back to them. Actively encourage them to tell their own stories. Include certain questions that are open-ended that would encourage people to share. That's the bottom line.

It's all about sharing and comfort. You're not trying to impress people by saying that you're well traveled, you have so much stuff, you're so much smarter than them. It has nothing to do with that. Instead, effective story telling is all about creating the safe emotional space that everybody can buy into. Always remember that. That is your goal.

If you lose sight of your goal, you're going to fail.

Chapter 15: Set A Date and Do It

Now that you have the information you need to step up your social skills, it's time to take action. I have laid out a systematic and methodical way that enables you to become more social. You will be able to step up your social skills through sheer practice. You need to do it over and over again until you get to the point where any kind of social interaction is comfortable to you. It's no longer intimidating. It's not something that you would actively avoid.

The moment somebody tells you that you have to speak in front of a crowd of strangers or you're going to meet somebody new and there might be something big on the line, you don't automatically break out in a cold sweat. Your mind doesn't snap into all sorts of delaying tactics. You're not rattling off a thousand and one reasons why you'd rather not do it. Instead, you look forward to it. You think back to the last success that you had and you can't wait to improve on it because you know that exercising your social skills is not much different from going to the gym and building up your muscles.

Sure, in the beginning, your muscles will feel sore. After all, you haven't put that much pressure on them, but as long as you keep going to the gym, your muscles get tighter, stronger and bigger. Same applies to your social skills. You have to test them. It's not always going to be pleasant. There might be some pain or discomfort involved, but that's how you get better.

Sure it's embarrassing when you fall flat on your face, those awkward silences can definitely suck, but the more you try, the higher the chance you will achieve some success. The more success you wrack up, the easier and easier it becomes for you. In fact, you may reach a point where there's really no chance that you'll fall flat on your face. You can pretty much write that out. Instead, the only challenge is whether this engagement will be better than the last one. In other words, you're looking to break new ground.

I know this sounds crazy and fantastical, but you will get there. It all boils down to a decision. You have to do it. In this chapter, I'm going to step you through the process of taking action on the information I shared with you in previous chapters. Let me be clear, all the best information in the world that enables you to do a truly great job with anything is not going to help you one bit if you don't implement them.

Of course, to take action, you have to set a date. You can't just jump in with both feet when you feel like it. That is a one-way ticket to failure. Doing things impulsively almost always leads to disappointment. Instead, you have to set a date when you will start. This is not as easy as you think.

Setting your start date is crucial

If you set up a start date that is too close to today, you're just going to freak yourself out. You see that date getting closer and closer and you're just too preoccupied with everything else that's going on in your life. After all, if you're anything like a typical person, you have all sorts of duties and responsibilities, tasks and obligations. There's just so many balls up in the air that you're juggling and this deadline you've set for yourself gets nearer and nearer. What do you think will happen?

It's not rocket science folks. You're going to freak out. You're going to feel that there's too much pressure. What happens when that date comes? You are not up to the job. You barely limp out of the gate and you fail. It's almost a foregone conclusion. Why? You've set up a start date that is simply too early.

Unfortunately, the other extreme is just as bad. Setting a start date that is too far in the future is sure to lead to disappointment as well. Why? You may seem like you have enough time to prepare, but here's the problem. If the start date is so far ahead, you're going to always find things to worry about in the here and now. You're always going to find new responsibilities, obligations, tasks, and other small stuff. Soon enough, your schedule is filled with the small stuff instead of you preparing for the start date. What do you think happens?

When the start date comes, you actually end up in the same position if you had set the start date too early. This is called Parkinson's law. It plays out every single time until and unless you choose to avoid it. Don't set the start date so far in the future. Set the right start date. It must be close enough to adequately prepare for, but not so close to the present date that it freaks you out.

Unfortunately, there is no answer that applies across the board. There's no one size fits all solution. You have to find the answer yourself because you are the most familiar with your set of circumstances. You know what you're working with. You know your past patterns.

Commit to starting on time

Now, this is the clincher. Setting the start date, as hard as it is, is just the tip of the iceberg. If you're able to do that and it's the right start date, congratulations. You have overcome many different hurdles.

Here's another one. You need to actually commit. This is not just another notation on your calendar. This is not a to do list that you conveniently overlook each and every time. You can't blow this off. When you commit, you're going to do it regardless of what happens. That's the kind of commitment you should hold yourself to. Even if you don't feel like it, you still do it. That's the kind of commitment that will help you truly take your social skills to the next level.

When that date comes, do it. This might mean meeting a new member of the opposite sex by going to a social space. This might mean using Tinder to find a date and actually meeting that person. This might mean setting up a business meeting on that date. Whatever form it takes, you need to do it and you need to do it on time.

You don't have to blast out of the gate

Here's an important piece of news for you. When that date comes and you need to get social at that time, you don't have to come out of there like a perfect social master. That's not going to happen. Don't beat yourself up with unrealistic expectations. Instead, approach the whole thing the way a student would. "Low and slow" is okay. You don't have to get massive results.

The good news is it's exactly like going to the gym. In the beginning, your muscles may be sore. You may not be able to lift all that much weight, but it doesn't matter. What matters is that you find yourself in that exact same gym at the exact same time tomorrow and the day after that, and the week after that. Week after week. Month after month. Year after year. That's how you make progress.

You may start out low and slow, but it doesn't mean you're going to stay there. You're going to scale up as things get easier and more familiar. As you are able to make people around you comfortable just as you are comfortable, things will scale up.

Conclusion

Social skills are crucial for any kind of success. We need other people to get anywhere in life. We need them for better relationships, piece of mind and emotional health. They need us as much as we need them. By paying close attention to the tips and tricks I shared in this book, you can go a long way in improving your social skills.

You have to always understand that there is only one person that can hold you back from the social successes you are otherwise capable of. This person spells his or her name this way: Y-O-U. That's right. Only you can hold yourself back. Don't let anybody tell you otherwise. You are smarter than you think. You are more social than you give yourself credit for. You have it in you. You just have to believe.

Please follow this book. Use the information in the sequence that I have laid out. That sequence is not an accident. It's there for strategic purposes. If you follow everything in precise order and you master each and every step, you will overcome your shyness. You will make more friends. You will, ultimately, have a greater impact on your world. I wish you nothing but the greatest love, happiness, and peace.

Access Your FREE Report

Thank you for downloading this book. As a way of showing my appreciation, I want to give you a **FREE REPORT** along with this book.

4 Social Skills That Help You Achieve Success In All Aspects Of Your Life!

http://geni.us/freesocialreport

This Free Report will teach you about-

- 4 Social Skills That Help You Achieve Success.
- Why Is It Important For Introverts To Socialize?
- Networking Tips For Shy People.
- Where To Meet New People.

Recommended Book

Self Confidence: Unleash Your Hidden Potential and Breakthrough Your Limitations of Confidence
(Available on Amazon)

You can access this book by visiting the link below-

http://geni.us/selfconfidence

This will teach you how to build up your self-confidence so you can achieve victories in all areas of your life.

Thank You

Made in the USA
Middletown, DE
26 January 2019